THE CONSC[...]

GU[...]

D0005960

Raising Girls

PROMOTE
SELF-ESTEEM

A mindful
approach to
raising a
strong, confident
daughter

BUILD
RESILIENCE

IMPROVE
COMMUNICATION

Erika V. Shearin Karres, EdD,
and Rebecca Branstetter, PhD

A adamsmedia

Avon, Massachusetts

Published by
Adams Media, a division of F+W Media, Inc.
57 Littlefield Street, Avon, MA 02322. U.S.A.
www.adamsmedia.com

Contains material adapted from *The Everything® Parent's Guide to Raising Girls, 2nd Edition* by
Erika V. Shearin Karres, EdD, copyright © 2011 by F+W Media, Inc., ISBN 10: 1-4405-1098-9,
ISBN 13: 978-1-4405-1098-4.

ISBN 10: 1-4405-9991-2
ISBN 13: 978-1-4405-9991-0
eISBN 10: 1-4405-9992-0
eISBN 13: 978-1-4405-9992-7

Printed in the United States of America.

10   9   8   7   6   5   4   3   2   1

Cover design by Stephanie Hannus.

This book is available at quantity discounts for bulk purchases.
For information, please call 1-800-289-0963.

Contents

Acknowledgments

There are many people I could thank for the opportunity to write this book, but I have to say that the two most important to thank are my daughters. You two have taught me more about raising girls than any course or book ever could. I am so blessed to have such amazing, spirited, funny, and warm little girls in my life! I couldn't do it alone, though; thanks to my husband, Steven. You are a fun-loving, smart, patient, kind, and gifted father to our girls, and I thank you for being on this parenting journey with me!

Introduction

As the parent or caregiver of a girl, you may really feel a strong desire to equip her to face the world's challenges without marring her wonder for it. You want your little girl to grow up healthy and safe and happy, and to be able to enjoy her childhood to the fullest. You want her to become a strong, capable, and independent-minded teenager with huge hopes and dreams and a will to succeed. Finally, you want her to blossom into a confident and successful young woman with the whole world at her fingertips.

You can't bubble-wrap your little girl—you know that—so what should you do? Whom can you ask for advice?

You start to feel a little frantic because even the "experts" you decide to go to—through your reading or on the Internet—seem to contradict themselves. All those programs and magazines entirely devoted to parenting offer nothing much that is new except new areas for serious concern. You didn't even know little girls could get depressed at age three or worry themselves sick over not having brand-name outfits to wear in kindergarten. The only thing you do know is that you love your daughter with all your heart, and that you will do anything to protect her.

Stop worrying. Stop searching far and wide for answers. Your love for your little girl is enough, and you already have all the answers. You, *only* you, know your daughter and how best to raise her. You know what you envision for her future. You really have within yourself all the skills it takes to raise a wonderful daughter, even in the turbulence and uncertainty of today. And thankfully, the tide seems to be turning in regard to the attitudes toward girls and young women. Your daughter has many more positive role models and messages of encouragement than any generation of daughters before.

This guide does not have "all the answers." Every girl is different and every parent is different. Rather than a prescription, this book is full of all kinds of great suggestions, hints, choices, and solutions gathered from research, readings, and the hands-on experience of parents just like you. *The Conscious Parent's Guide to Raising Girls* is going to be by your side every day with a menu of information, options, main points, and stories from which to choose whatever best fits your and your child's needs.

You truly are capable of raising the most wonderful daughter and of helping her become a young woman who is strong, independent, loving, and successful, even in these most difficult times. It starts with taking a step back and reflecting on your own parenting. The beauty of conscious parenting is that you do not have to strive to be all-knowing; you simply need to be more reflective on the parenting choices you make. By doing so, you can make conscious decisions that will help your daughter be herself and resist gender stereotypes, help her accept and appreciate her body, and help her develop the confidence she needs to take risks, be successful, and be safe in the world. You can help her prepare for healthy relationships, interesting and fulfilling work, and independence. It all starts with you, and believe it or not, you know what you want for your daughter's future—and for your own. Make your hopes and wishes come true. You can, and you will.

 **CHAPTER 1**

Conscious Parenting

Being a conscious parent is all about building strong, sustainable bonds with your children through mindful living and awareness. Traditional power-based parenting techniques that promote compliance and obedience can disconnect you from your children. Conscious parenting, on the other hand, helps you develop a positive emotional connection with your child. You acknowledge your child's unique self and attempt to empathize with her way of viewing the world. Through empathetic understanding and tolerance you create a safe environment where your child feels her ideas and concerns are truly being heard. When you find yourself in a stressful situation with your child, rather than reacting with anger or sarcasm, conscious parenting reminds you to instead take a step back, reflect, and look for a peaceful solution—one that honors your child's individuality and motivations.

This approach benefits all children, especially girls, who may be bombarded with mixed messages from society about how they "should" be. Your job as a parent of a daughter is to help her be the best she can be, by respecting her individuality and encouraging her to be true to herself. Society will send her many messages about how she should think, feel, and act, and you can be her guide along the way, providing empathy and encouragement as she learns and grows into a young woman.

Adopting the conscious parenting philosophy can relieve your stress and improve your child's self-image. The strong bond built between you and your child, along with your own calm, respectful attitude, will help her to develop positive behavior patterns. Parent-child conflicts over behavior can stem from an unfulfilled need your daughter may have. These needs often go unspoken, so having an open line of communication with your daughter is essential. If she feels heard, understood, and appreciated for her viewpoint, you will be able to partner with her to problem-solve any situation that arises. This does not mean you have to agree with her viewpoint every time, but it is helpful to seek understanding and empathize with her.

As a conscious parent, it is also important to be mindful of your own expectations of your daughter and not let them get in the way of her blossoming into who she is meant to be. Conscious parents do not try to mold their daughters into being a certain way, but rather set the stage for developing her strong self-image and self-confidence. By doing so, you are honoring her individuality and are less likely to have conflict and behavioral challenges arise.

The Benefits of Conscious Parenting

Conscious parenting isn't a set of rules or regulations that you must follow, but rather it is a system of beliefs. Conscious parents engage and connect with their children, using mindful and positive discipline rather than punishment. They try to be present when they're spending time with their children, avoiding distractions like TV and social media. Conscious parents respect their children and accept them as they are. The most important part of conscious parenting is building an emotional connection with your daughter so you can understand the underlying reasons for her behavior.

Conscious parenting is about listening with full attention, and embracing a nonjudgmental acceptance of yourself and your child. As you engage in the act of *becoming*, you will discover a heightened sense of emotional awareness of yourself and your child, a clearer self-regulation in the parenting relationship, and a greater compassion for yourself and your child.

Conscious parenting brings with it a number of benefits, including improved communication, stronger relationships, and the feeling of greater happiness and satisfaction in life. Some of these benefits appear more immediately, while others take some time to emerge. The benefits of conscious parenting and mindfulness are a result of making them a part of your daily life. With practice, conscious parenting becomes an integral part of who and how you are in the world, and will in turn become a central part of who your child is as well.

SELF-AWARENESS AND SELF-CONTROL

One of the first benefits of conscious parenting that you (and your daughter) will see is a heightened awareness of yourself and your inner life, including your emotions, thoughts, and feelings. As you become more aware of these various forces moving within you, you can begin to watch them rise without being at their mercy. For example, when you are aware that you are becoming angry, you have a choice about whether to act from that anger or attend to that feeling directly. You will start to notice the things that tend to set you off—your triggers—and you will begin to be able to anticipate your emotions before they have a hold on you.

Mindfulness is the practice of being attentive in every moment, and noticing what is taking place both inside and outside of you without judgment. It is the practice of purposefully seeing your thoughts, emotions, experiences, and surroundings as they arise. Simply put, mindfulness is the act of paying attention.

As you become more skilled at noticing the thoughts and feelings that arise, you will begin to notice them more quickly, maybe even before they start to affect your actions. This awareness is itself a powerful tool. It opens up the possibility to say, "Hey, I'm pretty mad right now," as opposed to yelling at somebody you care about because you were upset about something else. It can do exactly the same thing for your daughter, helping her to learn to communicate about her feelings rather than just react from that place of emotion. As with most things, children learn this best by seeing it modeled by the adults in their lives.

Often, you may notice that your emotions carry with them a sense of urgency. As you feel the impulse to do something arise within you, you will be able to see the forces driving that sense of "I need to do something." They could be, for example, the thoughts that come up as you watch your three-year-old put on her own shoes. Your mind might be buzzing with impatience, and the thought *I need to put her shoes on for her because she's taking forever* arises. When you notice this thought instead of immediately acting on it, you have some room to check in with yourself and act intentionally, instead of just reacting. This practice of noticing creates a certain amount of mental space in which you can deal with the thought or feeling itself rather than let it move you to act.

WELL-BEING

Conscious parents understand that all they do and say over the course of each day *matters*. It is a sense of the *now*, being in the present moment without regard or worry for the past or future. When you become more mindful, you may find that you become more accepting of the things in life that you can't change and experience less stress. The net result is greater satisfaction and enjoyment of whatever each day has to offer. This sense of well-being offers a satisfaction and contentment in knowing that we are who we are intended to be, doing precisely what we are designed for in the moment.

As human beings, we each possess the tools for contributing something of value. Assess your gifts and talents—those personality traits and skills that make you unique—and determine how to employ them to enhance your parenting. If you take a full accounting of yourself—good, bad, and indifferent—and *own* the sum total of your individual experience, you are taking the first step toward conscious parenting.

Empathy and Acceptance

The awareness you gain as a conscious parent has the practical purpose of redefining your perception of yourself and your compassionate understanding of your child. When you understand how your child experiences the world and how she learns, you can communicate in ways that really reach her. This largely happens through modeling, or teaching through example. Doing so allows you to pass on the values and lessons that are important to you, regardless of your beliefs.

If you are a mother, you may have empathy for your daughter's growing pains because you have personal experience from when you were growing up. As for fathers (and mothers, for that matter), one doesn't have to have walked in one's *exact* shoes to have empathy. You can still be an empathic listener to your daughter. All children want to feel understood, and being a good listener sends the message, "I may not get it exactly, but I am trying to understand because I care."

ACCEPTANCE AND VALIDATION

Your child relies upon you and your family to provide a solid foundation of self-esteem. Equipped with a strong sense of self-worth, your child will be better prepared to enter into a life that will likely present many challenges. Much of your time and energy will be expended on raising, counseling, and disciplining your child in ways that she will understand. It is important to also remember that the root of disciplining your daughter is teaching, not punishing. Your relationship will be more positive and balanced if you also take time to reinforce your love and appreciation of her gifts and talents.

Giving Your Daughter Your Full Attention

All too often people multitask their way through the day. This is a coping mechanism you have probably developed as a means of juggling the many projects, tasks, errands, and obligations that you are responsible for. Although it is a common approach to managing the multiple things you have to do, it splits your attention in ways that distract your mind and actually lessen the quality of your attention. In reality, heavy multitasking causes your work and social interactions to suffer because of how it divides your focus.

To avoid this becoming an issue between you and your child (and to make sure you're modeling the kind of focus and engagement you want your child to use as well), make sure to practice engaged listening when you are at home with your family. This means setting aside other distractions, making eye contact, and giving the speaker (in this case, your child) your full attention.

Even if you set down what you are doing and are looking at your child, check in with yourself. Is your mind focused on what she is saying, or is it still planning, scheduling, remembering, projecting, or worrying? It is very easy to only half-listen, and this can be especially true when it comes to listening to children.

> Multitasking is neurologically impossible. When you try to multitask, what you actually end up doing is rapidly switching between tasks. Each time you do so, you lose efficiency and concentration, so stop trying! Do one thing at a time so you can do it with your whole brain, then move on to the next.

The stories your child tells are not always relevant to your adult life. The idea behind active listening is not that you suddenly care about what everyone else brought to school for Show and Tell; it's that you care about your child, and she wants to tell you the funny, strange, or interesting things that she experienced that day. The important part of this interaction is that your child wants to share her joy, curiosity, and interests with you. She wants to interact with you and share parts of herself and her life with you, and this is one of the ways she can do that. Don't miss out on this gift, even if the subject itself bores you. You'll be surprised by the interest you may develop in these things as you listen to your child talk. When a person you love cares about something, it becomes easier to see that "something" through her eyes and come to appreciate it all the more.

Understanding Your Daughter's Behavior

From the moment your little girl was born (or perhaps even before then), her experience in the world has been shaped by societal expectations about how girls "should" be. From the first pink princess outfit she sees to the daily media bombardment of images promoting impossible beauty standards, your girl is receiving subtle and constant messages about how to behave "appropriately" as a girl. On the other hand, there are also images of powerful, smart, brave, and innovative girls and women in our society.

Your role as a parent is to help her be aware of these expectations and critical of stereotypes, and provide her with messages and opportunities to be true to herself.

No matter where you fall on the nature vs. nurture argument of raising a girl, you can help inspire your daughter to overcome negative stereotypes. The disparity between the way parents treat boys and the way they treat girls is often inadvertent. Awareness of gender inequalities is the key to change.

It is also important to enjoy and accept the daughter you have in front of you—her temperament, her gifts, and even her shortcomings, no matter where they fall on the gender spectrum. Is she sporty? Does she love pink and frilly clothing? Does she tend toward caring for others? Is she more of an independent soul? Is she a lover of literature? Science? Technology?

Being a conscious parent is not about trying to mold or change your daughter into your idea of how she *should* be (either in your mind or society's image); it's about creating conditions for your daughter to develop into the amazing individual she is *meant* to be, free from the binds of gender stereotypes.

Conscious parenting is a process that is as unique and individual as each family. Parenting in a mindful manner requires an authentic appreciation for your gifts and talents (and those of your child), as well as an understanding of how best to employ those gifts and talents to help your child grow to be a happy, successful member of society. Think of this style of raising your child as *parenting with grace*. Having a graceful approach means understanding the following:

○ There is safety in sameness and comfort in what is familiar.

○ In order to feel safe and comfortable, the child must have control.

Think about the times when your child appeared most content, comfortable, and at ease. Was she enjoying playing a solitary computer game? Was she alone in her bedroom, drawing whales and sharks? Or was she directing a play starring her siblings and friends? In these instances, was your child engaged in a favored, pleasurable activity? Was it a repetitive activity from which comfort is derived? And during this activity, did your child have control? The answer to these questions is likely yes.

Now, reverse the situations and remove the elements of safety, comfort, and control. Say the computer unexpectedly locks up and the video game is interrupted. A sibling won't turn down his music while your daughter is attempting to concentrate on the details of her marine life drawings. Or a friend decides she doesn't want to be "bossed" around by your child and opts out of their playtime. These situations are unexpected and unpredictable. Your child feels unsafe, uncomfortable, and out of control when the unpredictable occurs and wins out.

Your child may feel overwhelmed by the loss of control. She may act out in a variety of undesirable ways. But if you take a moment to understand what's going on, you'll realize that she has good reasons for her behavior and is doing the best she knows how in order to cope with the loss of safety and comfort. Her reaction is a logical progression of that escalation until she learns other coping strategies.

When you are present in your parenting, you understand this and you can communicate your understanding to your child. Your emotional attachment to your child means that you can let her know that you understand *why* she is behaving in a certain way, even as you work together to find a better way of reacting the next time.

Think of the areas in which your child is naturally gifted. Does her comprehension of computer programs exceed that of many adults? Does she enjoy describing the exact alignment of our solar system's planets, identifying each by its correct name, placement, and physical characteristics? Does she assume the personality traits of a favorite cartoon character with uncanny accuracy, down to mimicking lines of dialogue? Or does she have the quiet reverence to render amazing watercolors? These passions are the areas of talent to recognize and encourage as uniquely your child's own.

Your appreciation of your child's gifts and talents will make your home and family a place where she is unconditionally loved and understood. Many parents just like you have made this mindful-parenting commitment and can readily attest to the profound, loving impact it has made on their lives.

CHAPTER 2

Your Infant Daughter

Let's start from the beginning: Congratulations! You are the parent of a baby girl! Sure, you may have a few difficult days early on, but soon you'll get a handle on your daughter's daily needs. You may even have a schedule of sorts. At any rate, after a few weeks or months, you can get more sleep and your energy level will bounce back. You feel that the toughest part physically of having a baby is over—and you are right! Now it's time to solidify a strong emotional and mental connection with your daughter, one that will carry through the years.

Developmental Factors

Your little girl is growing by leaps and bounds during her first year. Every day she surprises you with something brand new she has learned. Your heart almost bursts with joy as you observe her curiosity about all kinds of new things. You hardly dare blink for fear you'll miss something. In fact, when you consider just how much she will develop during the next twelve months, you feel like just placing her on a blanket on the floor, watching her all day long, and letting a video record every little detail. As you soak up your daughter's quick advancement, it's helpful to be aware of the four main areas that are the most noticeable.

The best advice for any parent is to be alert, aware, and proactive. Whenever a new possible threat to a child is mentioned in the media, take the warning seriously. For example, examine your little girl's crib now. Several styles have recently been found to be unsafe (check for recalls on the Internet). Also look at the crib at your baby's caretaker's place, if your child spends nap/sleep time away from home.

ABILITY TO MOVE AROUND

Around the age of six months, your baby girl can lift up her head and roll over. She can sit up if you support her back, bounce, and begin to put some weight on her legs.

Six months later, your little girl can crawl, perhaps pull herself up to a sitting then standing position, and take a step. After another half-year has passed, she can walk, pick up a toy she dropped, and proceed up some steps if you hold her hand.

Your daughter's development from a helpless baby to a child who scoots around so fast you can hardly keep up with her passes so quickly that it seems like a new miracle occurs almost daily. More miracles occur in regard to her sight and hand movement.

VISION AND FINE MOTOR SKILLS

By the time your baby girl is six months old, she is able to follow a moving object—whether it is a twirling toy or you—with her eyes and can reach for the object. Once she manages to grab that object, her aim will be to bring it to her mouth. At the age of one year, she can grasp a small object and let go of it with ease. She can pick up a rattle with each hand and whack them together. Six months later, she can pile a few blocks on top of each other, turn a page in a big book, and start to show a preference for using one hand over the other.

Besides her growth spurts in locomotion and vision, your baby daughter also attains many new milestones in her auditory ability, comprehension, and oral communication skills.

HEARING AND SPEAKING

At around six months of age, a baby can recognize her parent's tone of voice. She will turn her head to track where sounds come from and say her vowels. What is especially touching to observe is that now she can not only smile but also laugh, chuckle, and squeal with delight. Six months later, she knows her name, knows basic household objects and their uses, and can babble to herself in her own language. She may even say a few recognizable words. At eighteen months, she can understand short sentences and has a vocabulary of up to twenty words. That burgeoning ability to interact verbally with others helps your little girl in the last big area of her development.

Although all babies exhibit the acquisition of their most important skills in a similar order—for example, babies learn to roll over before they sit up—the speed at which these skills are gained can vary enormously. A sudden change in the baby's environment can also slow her developmental rate. Your checkups with your pediatrician will help you gauge if she is on target (as there is a broad range) or if support is needed.

PLAYING AND SOCIALIZING

While at the age of six months your baby can be shy around strangers, she enjoys looking at herself in the mirror and playing peekaboo with you. Before long, however, she will learn to wave goodbye, clap her hands, and look for a toy that is hidden, thereby exhibiting the first signs of developing a memory. At one year, she will enjoy dropping objects or putting them into a box. She will like playing patty-cake and being around you and any other adult she knows and can snuggle with. Six months later, she will set out to explore her complete living quarters, use a spoon and cup, and alternate between being too clingy and wanting to be set down on the floor—now.

Be sure to take your little girl to her regular checkups and have her get the recommended immunizations. Always take a small notepad that is filled with questions that occur to you, dealing with your daughter's development, and even more important, to record what the pediatrician tells you. Many parents are in such a rush at the doctor's office that they do not remember later what they were told. A few pertinent notes will keep you on track.

As you can tell, the various skills that fall under the four broad developmental areas are only a partial list. Your baby girl needs to master many more abilities, and you, the parent or caregiver, want to be able to assist her in that process. How? It is simple—just tune in to your daughter's world. Consider keeping a list of her developmental milestones, either in a baby book or in a smartphone app.

Your Baby's World

For a moment, put yourself in your baby's position and realize just how much she has to learn and how quickly. There is not another period in her life when she has to amass such a mountain of knowledge and attain so many developmental milestones. She has to do it by herself, but you can help by providing her with what it takes to make her monumental task easier. Of course she continues to need all the basics: food, her little bed, and fresh diapers. Beyond that, there are other objects that help her develop her potential at the speed that is optimal for her.

BABYPROOFING

Before rushing to buy out the toy store, first babyproof your home by lying on the floor and examining the furniture, walls, and bric-a-brac for safety issues. Then cover the electrical outlets, remove any valuables, and pad the sharp corners of the coffee table and any other pieces of dangerous furniture. Crawl around and see what you have missed. Then stock up on baby toys that are safe, but do not introduce them to her all at once.

TOY BY TOY

One new toy at a time is sufficient. Let your little girl examine it, absorb its shape and color, handle it, and get familiar with it. Let her form an attachment to it and to you. Too many new things at once can overwhelm your little daughter.

As much as your baby needs stimulation from toys, you are your child's most important form of stimulation! Talking, singing, and playing interactive games with your daughter are the best ways to form a strong attachment with her. Encourage her when she is trying something new for the first time, like crawling, walking, or talking. It is your encouragement, praise, and smile that will spur her on as she learns. Slow down and take in your daughter during this precious and fleeting stage of her life. She will never be a baby again, so enjoy it!

Maintain a Routine (for You and Her)

When your baby girl was only a few weeks old, you entertained her with conversation and song, but it was primarily a one-sided process. Now that she is able to make sounds such as "da-da" and "ma-ma," you want to build on her newly learned early speech capabilities and encourage them as best you can.

One quick way to do this is to incorporate books into her life. It works best if you do the following:

- Set a regular time for reading to her. This time may be right before her nap or before she goes to bed at night.

- Have books on hand that are geared to her age. Your neighborhood bookstore or public library has a list of the best books for babies and small children.

- Read the same book to her over and over, allowing her to point to the ducks or the kittens as you read about them, so that before long she can "read" the story back to you.

- As far as music, you probably have already found out that your little girl likes certain songs played at a low volume as her favorite lullabies. Now is the time to get a songbook and sing your childhood favorites with her. Have her sit on your lap and sing to your heart's content.

To your baby's ears, your voice will sound better than that of the most acclaimed singer in the world. Again, start with an easy song or a well-known rhyming ditty. Before too long, your baby will clap along, bounce on your lap, or hum along with you. What makes the reading and singing habit especially beneficial for your little daughter is that even if your day gets crazy, the established routine will show her all is well anyway. Babies, as much as they tend to make us overturn our regular schedules, thrive on the sameness of something they enjoy.

There will inevitably be times when schedules and routines change, such as when you are going back to work or when there is a new caregiver. But certain activities, like the customary twenty minutes with you or a caregiver that are devoted to books and/or music, are like a handrail for your little girl. She can move ahead in her development knowing that she can still rely on these daily interactions.

It is easy for new parents to want to take a mental break by turning on the TV, checking social media, texting, or browsing the web while their new baby plays. But by doing so, you are missing opportunities to interact and be fully present with your baby girl. Even as infants, children are learning about how the world works, and your distraction may be signaling to her that adults do not give full attention. Of course, take needed breaks, but do your best to do so when your child is sleeping or in the care of another.

FUN TIME AS A ROUTINE

Even when a parent is a full-time parent, unavoidable changes can occur in the household, such as a relative coming to live with the family, a parent going on a business trip, or a move to a bigger home. Your little girl will weather these changes much better if her fun times with you stay exactly the same, and you will feel content that while the surroundings or circumstances of your family are in flux, her world's foundation remains solidly in place.

Her Care and Needs

As your baby grows, so do her requirements and needs. They do not become more difficult, only different. No longer do you feel as if you have to hover over her every minute. At other times, you can carry your little girl with you from room to room in her baby seat or in a baby carrier such as a sling. It is then that you notice she's heavier. Her weight increases along with her length, and both change very quickly during her infancy. Although baby boys grow faster than girls during the first seven months, girls take off after that and continue to grow more rapidly until about age four. No matter how speedily your daughter grows, her needs continue to increase in two vital areas—the physical and the emotional—and her care requires that you keep both aspects of her development in mind.

PHYSICAL NEEDS

On the physical front, your baby daughter outgrows her outfits often as fast as you can replace them. You will also notice the change in her body's proportions. During her first year, her head grows almost to its adult size. A baby's body shape changes because her various parts grow at different rates. Although her head is disproportionately large at birth—as compared to the rest of her body—her body catches up before too long. During early childhood, her arms and legs grow faster than her trunk, but the whole growth process balances itself out thereafter.

From the first time you take your baby girl out in the world, you will likely experience others commenting on her outfits and appearance. Consider balancing comments about her looks with other aspects about her ("And she is such a happy baby, too!"). If this feels too awkward, you can always just say "Thank you" and later make a positive comment on your own not related to your daughter's looks. Starting when she is young will give you more comfort in handling the many comments you will get on her looks in the future, and send her the message that her identity is more than just her appearance.

Your little girl's appetite increases, as does her wish for, and ability to digest, solid foods. Once she is four months old, you may start introducing her to one or two teaspoons of cereal or puréed fruit or vegetables. Ask your pediatrician what he recommends for your baby girl; no two babies are ever the same. But before long she will indicate by her facial expressions if the jar of split peas tasted as good to her as the applesauce.

EMOTIONAL NEEDS

Your baby daughter may be able to say "Down," meaning "Put me down," by the time she is one year old, but she always wants you close by. So keep spending as much time as you can with her and continue to hug, kiss, and show your love for her. Also, when you promise her you will do something, follow through. If you have to be separated from your little girl during the day, make sure to reattach to her emotionally each evening. A warm and trusting relationship with your daughter is a requirement that takes a little effort every day but brings enormous benefits. Babies who are neglected emotionally grow up to crave attention at all costs, often cannot cope with frustrating events, and may even show a delay in their overall development, according to studies backed by the American Medical Association's *Encyclopedia of Medicine*.

Even if you work at a job with long hours, you can meet the emotional needs of your baby daughter. Every evening when you come home, focus on her first thing. Turn your phone off, or put it on Do Not Disturb or Airplane Mode, and give her your full attention. Many research studies prove that infants do very well with more than one primary caregiver. All that is required is a person who is loving and consistent and fills in capably for you while you are gone.

A 2015 study from Harvard Business School professor Kathleen McGinn, Harvard Business School researcher Mayra Ruiz Castro, and Elizabeth Long Lingo of Mt. Holyoke College showed that daughters of mothers who worked—either part-time or full-time—grow up to be successful in the workplace and hold egalitarian gender views as adults. This is not to say daughters of employed moms are "better," only that working moms can shed some of the "mom guilt" if they do elect to (or need to) go back to work.

BALANCING YOUR NEEDS AND YOUR DAUGHTER'S NEEDS

The decision about when parents should go back to work can be an emotional one. In the United States, with so little legally mandated time given to new parents to be with their newborns, it is no doubt that going back to work can also be a financial and practical decision. The most important thing to remember is that no matter if or when you return to work, you are making the best decision you can. Letting go of guilt for staying home or for returning to work will go a long way for your own emotional well-being. A happy parent, no matter what the work situation is, is better equipped to be present for a child than an unhappy parent.

As with so many aspects of parenting, your baby's care becomes easier the older she gets. Her needs are less difficult to meet when she is able to express what she wants or what is bothering her. Sometimes, however, even after she has learned to say a few words, she still cannot tell you exactly what is wrong. Teaching your infant baby sign language has been shown to increase her ability to communicate and understand. Learning a few basic words like *more*, *pain*, and *eat* will help you understand why she may be fussing.

The Fussy Baby

Not all babies are placid and easily entertained and looked after during their first year. Some babies have such fine-tuned systems that they resemble extremely complicated mechanisms that can have many breakdowns. So you, the parent, have a lot on your plate, trying to adjust to a newborn baby with a high susceptibility to colds, earaches, or the flu, or one who has allergies, for example. You find yourself going to the pediatrician every week and constantly filling the prescriptions she gives you. Then you try to figure out how to make your daughter swallow the medicine, which, of course, she detests.

Or your baby may experience almost constant episodes of crying that are not due to an obvious illness. This type of baby is called "fussy" because she can cause a constant fuss, and these periods of crying do not abate even when you try the usual means of comforting her, such as feeding her, changing her diaper, or just cuddling her. What is worse, the periods of excessive screaming are more prolonged in the evenings when you are exhausted, having done a full day's work running the household or the office. Therefore, your fussy little girl presents an extra challenge, and one you may not have counted on, but you can manage it by using the following measures:

O Keep a record of when the irritable periods occur in your baby's day. What preceded them?

O Observe what she does while she's crying. Does she draw up her feet or otherwise indicate that her tummy hurts?

O Do not feed the baby every time she cries. Many fussy babies have immature digestive tracts, and a bloated stomach can make the condition worse.

O Most pediatricians use the word *colic* to describe the spasmodic pain that may very well be the cause of your little girl's fussiness. Talk to your daughter's doctor about whether or not she may have colic.

But no matter what the doctor's diagnosis is, your baby is not a happy camper. Soon you will find to your dismay that you are not a happy camper either. The good news is that your little girl will likely outgrow the condition by the time she is six months old, although some babies—just like some adults—have a more sensitive digestive system that may be theirs for life. So while your daughter suffers from this common but harmless colicky state that occurs in roughly one in ten infants, you want to do what you can to help her feel better.

Some things you can try include:

O Taking her for a ride in your car

O Playing some soothing music

O Putting her face-down on your knees while stroking her back

O Giving her a pacifier

O Rocking her in a rocking chair

Know that simply waiting until she gets older will also help, especially if you turn to your network of family and friends and share your concerns.

Draw on Your Network

Being a parent to a baby girl—whether she is the calm or the fussy type—is much easier if you have a network of other people who can come in and relieve you when your nerves get frayed. Many experts warn parents not to get too exhausted because exhaustion makes even easy baby chores, such as feeding or bathing, much more difficult. Therefore, have your phone handy. Have on speed dial all those people who can help you not only with the chores related to your infant but also with bringing in groceries and lifting your mood. Text simple questions; e-mail more complicated ones. Revel in the knowledge that your sisters, brothers, mom, and dad circle around you more closely now. Ask them for help.

Taking care of yourself makes you better able to take care of your girl. If you begin to get overwhelmed and tired, consider outsourcing household tasks like laundry, cleaning, and getting groceries if you have the means. There are a number of professional services that can help, such as online food delivery and laundry pickup.

ENJOY BABY JOYS

Enjoy being the center of your extended family's attention; be sure to inform each member of your little daughter's progress. Don't think you are shamelessly using them when you ask them to pick up the dry cleaning, make a run to the grocery store, load the dishwasher, and bring in the diapers.

Imagine a new mother whose baby girl goes through a relatively easy few weeks and then develops a stretch of irritability. Imagine her calling her parents before she and her partner are at their wits' end. Her family could bring home-cooked meals to her and take dirty laundry away and return it washed and folded. Neighbors and other parents may stop by for a chat, and they might have good suggestions (or a sympathetic ear!) for challenges that are arising.

ASK FOR HELP

Babies respond well to different calming techniques on different days, although not according to what you have in mind. Sometimes just putting your baby into the loving arms of another person—your grandmother, uncle, or cousin—distracts her enough to be able to sleep.

You can be a hero, but not if it means you feel as though you have to shoulder all the responsibilities that come along with an infant girl. To use an analogy, when on a plane in an emergency, you must put on your oxygen mask before assisting others! The same concept applies with your baby. Ask someone for help before you collapse from fatigue or reach the end of your rope.

When your baby's well-being is at stake, don't go it alone. You have to ask other people to assist you. You cannot drive yourself until there is nothing left in you. That is why you must also call on another network— your close and personal one.

FRIENDS

Remember your friends, no matter how far away. Keep in touch with them by texting them a picture of your baby girl. Ask your friends who have children questions as they come up. Experienced parents are usually more than happy to share their wisdom. Consider joining an online parents group if you have time. Even if the other parents don't have the "answers" for your daily challenges, sometimes just knowing that others are going through the same struggles can be a source of comfort.

PRACTICE SELF-CARE

It is also important to tend to your own needs. Make time for the things that recharge you—yoga, reading, taking walks, watching a favorite show—whatever relaxes you. You will be better able to take care of your daughter if you take care of yourself.

The biggest part of your close and personal network is your relationship with your own body. Breathe deeply, stretch, and start exercising. Your muscles will be grateful to you, your pants will fit better, and your energy level will skyrocket. Your little girl will look up to you as she watches you and even tries to imitate you. You and your spouse can then enjoy all aspects of being a wonderful family. If you are a single parent, you should be extra proud of the way you are evolving and getting better/stronger every day.

Important Points to Consider

Regardless of your views on nature vs. nurture in shaping gender roles, there are some universal principles that you will want to take into account, even when your daughter is an infant:

○ Gender stereotypes begin early—in clothing, toys, and the comments you make or will receive about your little girl. Small gender differences can grow into troublesome gaps when stereotyping is left unchecked.

○ While there is nothing wrong with people noticing how adorable your little girl is, take care to counterbalance comments with messages about her great traits that have nothing to do with her appearance.

○ The first year of your daughter's life is exciting and awe-inspiring but also exhausting and, at times, bewildering. Take care of yourself by asking for help, taking needed breaks, and cultivating self-care. The more rested and recharged you are, the better a parent you will be for your little girl.

○ Establish daily rituals such as reading to her, playing with her when you get home, and being silly and fully present with her when you are home.

○ Treat your decision to go back to work or stay at home with the same loving kindness you would for a friend. Parents have to make difficult choices, and the best choice is the one that you have made. Being content with your decision will free up mental and emotional energy to enjoy parenting your daughter.

 **CHAPTER 3**

Your Toddler Daughter

As your little girl grows older and becomes a toddler, looking after her becomes easier in some ways and more difficult in others. First, her increasing size makes her less fragile to handle. Second, she has learned to communicate with you through words, so she can better tell you what she's feeling. On the other hand, she is also learning to assert her independence, her new favorite word might be "No!" and she may dig in and have more tantrums than ever before. While tantrums can be challenging, they are also a rich opportunity for teaching your daughter emotional and behavioral self-regulation skills. They are great times to employ patience and mindfulness techniques to keep yourself calm, confident, and communicative.

Interacting Socially

One option you have is to widen the circle of interactions for your little girl. Up until now, this circle may have included only the parents, other close relatives, and/or the babysitter or caregiver. But now your little girl is ready to meet new people—her peers. For that reason, you might want to find an appropriate playgroup in your area.

In moments when your toddler is digging in and asserting her newfound independence and voice, you may find yourself becoming frustrated. To avoid power struggles, instead of reacting with stubbornness of your own or anger, take a deep breath and remind yourself that stubbornness is persistence and determination in disguise, and these are good things! This reframing can take the edge off frustrating moments. Then you will be calmer and better equipped to teach her how to manage her strong feelings.

Of course, if your daughter already spends the time you are at work in daycare or preschool, she may already have a playgroup. In that case, just add visits to the park and the playground, with you choosing carefully what types of play equipment your little girl is ready for. Keep in mind that toddlers have mastered many skills and enjoy playing with all sorts of toys. They can:

○ Climb up stairs—with two feet to a step—and benches, and back down.

○ Throw and kick a ball and retrieve it.

○ Show a preference for a favorite stuffed animal or toy.

○ Begin to use pretend play, such as putting a baby doll to bed, using tools to "fix" things, "feeding" stuffed animals, and "driving" cars around.

○ Build towers with blocks or Legos.

○ Ride a tricycle or a balance bike (a small, two-wheeled bike with no pedals).

Give your daughter a chance to try out her new play skills in a group setting. If you are a stay-at-home parent, however, and your little girl hasn't been exposed to many other children, you need to go more slowly. Introduce other little girls and boys to your daughter one at a time and keep play periods short to start. Many parents of toddlers form informal groups that meet, for example, two times a week, on a rotating basis. While the parents watch and visit, the small children play alongside each other or—as they mature—with each other.

Sometimes the children in a playgroup are older than your little girl; they may be rowdier, more demanding, even aggressive. Make sure the other little girls and boys are the types of children you want your little girl to emulate. You do not want her suddenly coming home saying bad words and hitting other children. Once you investigate what is going on, you will find that the other toddlers are not "bad"; it's just that no one has taken the time to teach them how to behave with other children.

There is some value in helping your daughter navigate these challenges, as she can learn skills such as assertiveness and help-seeking when problems arise. If you find her emulating unwanted behaviors, or she does not want to be part of the group anymore, the best thing you can do is express your concerns and reasons for leaving one playgroup and joining another. You already have much to do. Raising your little girl is a full-time job that fills whatever hours you have available, especially during the year from age two to age three.

If your daughter is having trouble in a group, step back and reconsider if she is ready for that particular group. For now, she may be better off with one-on-one playdates, which will give you time to help her learn positive group behavior.

The Terrific Twos

The reason for the terrible-twos perception was that many parents did not understand the normal stages of their child's development. At approximately two years of age, a child sees her world opening up with so much on the horizon that she cannot yet have. By then she has also learned that she can manipulate her parents by simply showing her displeasure—and the more obviously the better. Now she can use many words, but she doesn't necessarily understand their meanings. She is likely good at making her needs known. Plus, she is filled with questions and fires them off, one after the other. Also, while she has developed either left- or right-hand dominance by now and can undo her buttons and untie her shoes, she cannot yet redo her buttons or tie her laces, nor can she do other things that seem so simple to adults. So she is boiling over with frustration and impatience.

You may feel like ever since your little girl turned two, she has refused to do everything you tell her. Age two is a hard time for a child and her parents. Remember, she is not intentionally trying to be rebellious or defiant. She is just trying to express her growing independence, but she doesn't yet have adequate verbal skills to do so. Know that this won't last and that your little girl will outgrow this phase.

BE PREPARED

None of these characteristics is negative, however, unless the parent is not prepared. In fact, your little girl's demanding attitude and hurry-up manner are an opportunity to teach her how to manage negative feelings and act acceptably. All you have to do is expect her increased impatience, demands, and questioning and have a plan for how to deal with them. Slowly but surely, you will make progress with her.

What helps is that by now your daughter has learned to follow simple instructions. Therefore, make your instructions to her as simple and to the point as you can and expect them to be followed. No elaborate explanations need to be given about why you want her to drink her milk or get her coat; you can simply say, "Milk helps you grow strong" or "We wear coats when it is cold." In years to come you can give more detailed reasons for your instructions and rules, but now is too early for your little girl to understand whatever deeper implications there might be. Keep it simple.

If you give directions to your little girl in a kind but firm tone, you will get results. So, do not start screaming or moping over your hurt feelings when she balks. Your daughter does not mean to upset you. She is just going through a stage. Also there is no need for you to jump every time she expresses a wish. Calmly do what seems reasonable, after explaining to her that she has to ask nicely and not be demanding. Also, help her understand that raising her voice will not make you run to her side unless she is hurt. Only then is it all right—even necessary—to scream.

There are several practices that can help ensure the terrible twos turn into the terrific twos. First, be forewarned and do not take the sudden disagreeableness in your little girl as a sign you have made a mistake. Take it as an opportunity to expand your parenting skills. Many parents have tried the following hints and found that they work, if you use them on a consistent basis:

○ Avoid asking her a question that can be answered with "No," such as, "Do you want to wear the blue top?"

○ Give her two choices: "Would you like to wear the blue top or the yellow one?"

○ Have a regular routine for naps, meals, and so on, and try to stick to it each day.

○ If there are two things she needs to do, allow her to decide which she wants to do first, as in, "Do you want to pick up your toys first or take your bath first?"

Various other methods may occasionally work for parents of a little girl caught in the throes of the confrontational twos, but calmness and consistency always work—after a while. So keep at it.

PARENTING GROWTH

Discuss with other mothers and fathers what works for them and take notes. If you have an acquaintance with an exceptionally well-behaved three-year-old, ask for her cell phone number. An answer to your quick "help me" text can get you back on track. Also remember what you've tried that has had the best result for you. Then roll up your sleeves, feel confident in your parenting, and enjoy this terrific time in your daughter's life. She is becoming quite a little person now with a preference to play imaginatively and interact with you and others. As a mom or dad of a toddler girl, you will marvel at the funny things she is saying and doing as she develops her own unique personality.

In the process of rearing your daughter, you continue to grow as well. The more she challenges you with her developmental stages—some smooth, some rocky—the more chances you have to be resourceful and draw out innate parenting abilities you never even knew you possessed.

Your Girl Learns to Listen

One goal of parenting is to enable your child to learn from others. That is the reason for teaching your little girl one of the most important skills she can possess: how to listen and listen well. Once she has mastered this skill, all other childhood tasks will be so much easier for her to grasp and for you to teach.

One thing that can get in the way of your little girl's learning to listen is the TV. So often this appliance becomes a second parent. In too many households, it is turned on the moment someone gets up or comes home, or it is used as a tool to soothe or distract children when they are fussy or bored, or when the parent needs a break. Yet unlike a mom or a dad, TV never demands anything of a child. It is filled nonstop with changing images, music, and bright colors, but it does not require your child's full attention.

Even if you do not have the TV on constantly, being exposed to it for a few hours daily—or being exposed to lots of screen time, even if age-appropriate—tends to draw your baby girl's focus away from the voice of a parent or caregiver. Then she may start to tune out her mom's or dad's messages. Using screens to placate your child may work well in the short run, and give you a needed break, but the message you are sending your toddler is that she does not need to be bored, wait patiently, or experience negative feelings, because she can just be entertained and distracted instead. Some screen time can be appropriate, and even beneficial for learning, so long as it is not the go-to fix when your daughter is fussy.

GOOD LISTENING SKILLS

By now, you likely have a good sense if your daughter has trouble listening and following directions. If she tends to comply with your instructions after one or two repetitions, she likely has some solid listening skills. If you find that you are repeating yourself over and over again and she is not complying, she may need some support. In order to teach your daughter good listening skills, you will need to first check if it is a listening issue or a follow-through issue.

Start by giving your daughter a clear, one-step direction with a desirable outcome, such as, "Get your shoes so we can go to the park" or "Open the pantry for some crackers." Then add a second step, such as "Get your shoes and your coat so we can go to the park," and see if she can follow the two steps. If she cannot, then break down your instruction into one thing at a time. Do not automatically assume not following through on directions is non-compliance! She may not have processed all of your direction, or you may not have had her full attention to begin with.

If she is able to follow two- or three-step directions for desired tasks but does not do so for undesired tasks, then the issue may be not listening but follow-through. In this case, you may need to order your directions from least desired to most (e.g., "First brush your teeth and then we'll read a special story" or "Put your books away and then we can have a snack together"). Allowing her to choose the order of two undesired tasks can also help with compliance (e.g., "Do you want to eat your peas or carrots?" or "Which do you want to do first—brush your teeth or wash your face?"). If she does not make a choice, you can tell her that you will make a choice for her. This strategy helps boost her independence while still sending the message that she needs to comply.

CLEAR VOICE, CLEAR INSTRUCTIONS

While you are teaching your little girl to listen better and to follow through on instructions, you have to speak clearly, especially when you proceed to tell her to do more than one thing. For important directions, make sure that background noises such as music and the television are off. You may need to slow down your instruction and emphasize key words as well (e.g., "*First* eat your vegetables, *then* you get dessert" or "Get your *brown* shoes, please").

Of course, you must model good listening. When she tells you something, concentrate on her story. Put down any distractors such as your phone or laptop and be fully present. Give good eye contact and answer her questions, even if she peppers you with them. Even better, alternate the questioning and listening. She asks you something and you respond carefully. Then you ask her something and expect a complete answer from her—as much as she can give you one. If she cannot, she may not have the language skills to express herself, so give her a multiple-choice option (e.g., "Did I say we are going to the grocery store or to the train station first?"). Working on listening can be a fun game for you and your daughter, and allow you an opportunity to hear all her developing questions and ideas about the world!

Next, work on having her listen to what someone else says. Take her to story time at the library, and ask her to listen to the narrator carefully. On the way home, ask her what the story was about, and listen to her tell what she remembers. At her age, remembering one or two details is age appropriate. If she says she doesn't remember anything, jog her memory by asking questions (e.g., "What did that monkey in the story do at the beach?"). You can do the same thing at bedtime when you read to her, and you can go back and re-read to find interesting information she may have missed the first time. With practice, she will learn to listen better.

Tantrums and Strategies to Cope

Even if you have made a point of raising a good listener, there are always a few times when even the best-behaved child does not hear her mom or dad. Most often that happens when your little girl had a bad day or she is overtaxed from learning something new. Maybe it was filled with all sorts of frustrations. Suddenly she does something she has never done before. She throws a fit—otherwise known as a tantrum. These emotional eruptions can come out of nowhere or be a huge reaction to something you think is a minor problem. These outbursts can be frustrating and draining for the parents, but with consistency, determination, and understanding, even the worst tantrums can be overcome.

TANTRUMS

Tantrums can come on suddenly and seemingly for no apparent reason. But you, the conscious parent, will know how to handle the situation, because you will be seeking to understand the underlying motivation for your daughter's behavior. Again, as with most parental quandaries, once you know what a tantrum is and why it occurred, you have practically disarmed it. A tantrum is most often an outburst of bad temper in which your little girl may throw herself on the floor, yell for no immediately apparent reason, and bang her fists and kick like crazy.

According to Kay Albrecht, founder of HeartsHome Early Learning Center, temper tantrums erupt because the toddler cannot express herself as well as she would like to, even though her vocabulary might be as large as 300 words. What makes parents especially frustrated is that no matter how many times they tell their child to stop having a tantrum and calm down, even when they raise their voices, she will not. Later, when they ask their little girl what that was all about, she probably is not able to tell them because she has been on frustration overload. So understand that this is a tough time for your girl and for you, but losing your own temper won't help matters.

Never spank a child who has a temper tantrum. First, it does not work because she is unreachable during the tantrum, and second, she will then be encouraged to continue to have a tantrum—but only when you are not present. Use other methods to calm her down.

It sometimes works to simply ignore a tantrum when it occurs at home. Just steel yourself, go about your work, and ignore the little tantrum thrower. Be in her presence, though, so she is not alone with her big feelings. You can putter about the room while she throws her fit. Periodically acknowledge her frustration and try to talk to your little girl (e.g., "I know you're upset because you can't have a Popsicle right now. When you're through being upset, come and sit with me, and we'll discuss it." Or, "I see you are very angry. Let me help you calm down. Let's do deep breaths together before we chat about it.").

But when the tantrum occurs in a public place, ignoring it won't work very well. Therefore a different method has to be used. If her temper outburst happens while you are shopping at the grocery store or when you are walking in the park together, do the following:

1. Stop whatever you are doing and remove her from the public place. You may have to carry her—kicking and screaming—to the car. Do it anyway.

2. Help her calm down. You know your child best—does she need a hug, some distraction, music, or deep breaths? Or does she need to "fuss it out" and cry for a few minutes before she is ready to calm down?

3. When she has calmed down, tell her that you will try the outing again another day.

4. The next time you go out, set the stage for success. Tell her what you expect (e.g., keeping her body calm and peaceful, and using her words at the park) and the consequences if she throws a tantrum (e.g., leaving the park).

5. Do exactly what you said—if she does not throw a tantrum, praise her for what she did well, specifically (e.g., "I like how you used your words when you were angry" or "Good job telling me you were sad when you didn't get a Popsicle at the park"). If she throws another tantrum, leave the outing and try again another day.

6. Think of tantrums as teachable moments. We shouldn't expect two- or three-year-olds to have fully developed coping and communica-

tion skills. Your little daughter will learn how to act and express herself without causing an uproar, little by little, day by day, with your support.

TIME-OUTS AND TIME-INS

Many parents use time-outs with toddlers who have tantrums or refuse to listen. The concept of the time-out is that the toddler will stop what she is doing—literally take "time out" from her activity—think about the bad or inappropriate behavior she has just displayed, and be coached on other ways to respond next time. Time-outs are easily adaptable to any location. All you need is a chair, a corner, or a sofa. When your daughter has a tantrum, you can have her sit in the designated time-out spot and stay there until you tell her that her time-out is over. Some parents recommend a minute of time-out for every year of age. Two or three minutes can seem like a very long time for your child to sit by herself and can have an effect on her. Although it may take a long period for the time-outs to work, your little girl will catch on if this consequence is carried out consistently.

It is important to remember that your daughter's "misbehavior" is likely a signal that her coping skills are not developed enough for her to express her feelings of disappointment, anger, or frustration, so she is acting out in the only way she knows how. Time-outs should be used not as a punishment but as an opportunity to help her "reboot." You want to send the message that her big feelings are okay, and you are there to help her deal with them appropriately.

It should be noted that time-outs are not always successful for all children, especially extra-sensitive children. A child who has misbehaved or is in the throes of a tantrum may be experiencing strong and scary feelings. To put her in a time-out may seem like you are abandoning her with her out-of-control feelings. It may also inadvertently send her the message that anger is not okay, and she is getting punished for her feelings.

Messages about anger and gender start young. Some studies show that adults tend to perceive infant girls as "nice and happy" and male infants as "upset and angry," and many exhibit the "sugar and spice and everything nice" bias. Toddler girls are often expected to have more self-control than boys. These perceptions can inadvertently teach young girls that being angry is not appropriate or polite. Yet unchecked anger can lead to other problems, like worries, sadness, or acting out in other ways. From an early age, girls (as well as boys) should be told that anger is a feeling they have a right to experience and express. You may find it helpful to say, "It's okay to be angry, but it's not okay to [hit Mommy/throw your toys/etc.]."

Many parents prefer a "time-in," in which the parent accompanies the child to a designated place and helps her calm down. However, there is no point in even trying to reason with your daughter and have a talk with her until she is calm. She is not in a place to receive instruction. Think about times when you have been extraordinarily upset—reason likely got you nowhere until you calmed down. Instead, tell her you are there to help her calm down, and then once she is calm, you can discuss the misbehavior together. Save the long lectures; she is too young to hear them. Keep it short and simple: Describe the misbehavior, label and acknowledge a feeling, and provide an alternative behavior (e.g., "You hit your sister when she took your toy. It's okay to be angry, but it's not okay to hit. Next time, ask me to help."). Then ask her to repeat what she will do next time before ending the time-in.

TRUST PARENTING INSTINCTS

During this frustrating phase of raising your daughter, you need to trust yourself. You have already come so far in parenting this precious human being. Now build on that trust and stay strong. Gone are the early days when your little girl was like an appendage to you. Now she is coming more and more into her own, and it is you who must cut the cord. Stop feeling bad when your daughter gets disagreeable; this is not about you. It is her attempt to learn how to grow up and thrive. With each new skill she masters, she will feel more productive and proud. Do not stand in her way by denying her new achievements. Allow her to conquer all the challenges of being a toddler. She will make so much progress with you being loving and firm and expecting the best results in a timely manner.

Potty Training

There are many methods for toilet training; some focus on a speedy switchover and some condone making it a more gradual process. But whatever training method you choose, remember that every child is different, with a unique personality and rate of development.

Build some excitement for the process with your daughter. Tell her that her body is smart and knows how to get rid of waste. But just like you put trash in the trashcan, she has to put her body's waste in a special place: the potty. Take your daughter with you to buy the new potty-chair and let her choose which model she prefers. Having a say will create excitement over the potty and make your daughter more interested in using it. You could also get your daughter a book on potty training so she will have an idea of what to expect, or have your daughter watch you or an older sibling use the potty so she can have an understanding of the process.

The American Academy of Pediatrics suggests waiting until two years of age to potty train a child, but watch your child for signs of readiness (an awareness of needing to go, the motor skills to dress and undress herself, the cognitive ability to understand directions) and interest in potty training. Some children may be ready to train before two years, and some may need more time.

There are several potty-training methods you can use, but you'll want to use the one that you are most comfortable with. Whatever your decision is, be consistent and know the following steps can help you:

O Explain to your daughter the functions of her body.

O Use the correct terminology for her body parts.

O Have her help you with the cleanup when she makes a mess.

O Motivate her to be part of this wonderful new adventure.

O Be consistent and patient. Potty training is a process.

As the parent of a girl, the most important gender-specific potty-training tip to remember to tell your daughter is to wipe from front to back, thereby helping to prevent any bacteria from infecting the sensitive skin of the vagina. Also, use correct terminology for her private parts. This way, she can specifically identify which parts of her body are hurting (e.g., rashes, soreness), if needed.

It may seem too early to start lessons about body consent, but you can plant the seeds now for your daughter to understand that her body is her own. Use potty training and bathing as opportunities to teach her to say yes or no to others touching her private parts. For example, ask her if she wants to wipe or clean her vagina or if she is okay with you doing it for her. This will give her a voice early on and teach her that she has a choice about being touched.

Important Points to Consider

The toddler years are when you will really begin to see your daughter's personality blossom. Along the way, you will no doubt experience frustration as she learns to use her voice and independence, but it can also be a fun time. Consider the following points as you navigate these early years:

O Remember that your daughter's newfound ability to say "no" and protest is part of a normal developmental phase, and is really the first step toward acquiring good traits, such as persistence and determination.

O Avoid labeling your daughter's misbehavior and tantrums as "bad." Reframe tantrums as opportunities to teach self-regulation and coping skills when she has negative feelings or things don't go as she expected them to.

O Be aware of gender stereotypes about little girls and expression of anger. Your daughter has every right to feel and express anger. If she is expected to always be in control and be "nice," her anger may be stifled, and down the road she may be at risk for unhealthy expressions of this strong emotion.

○ How you manage misbehavior and tantrums will likely depend on your daughter. You may like time-outs, or you may rely on time-ins. You know your daughter best, so trust your instincts.

○ As a conscious parent, just knowing about stereotypes can help you be more aware of the choices you make in purchasing items for your daughter. Consider buying a range of toys, not just typical "girl" toys.

○ During big transitions, it is important to be patient and take each day as it comes. Do not expect overnight success. Celebrate little steps along the way with your daughter.

 **CHAPTER 4**

Your Preschool Daughter

The joy of raising a girl grows constantly, because there's so much more she has to learn about the world and so much more you want to teach her. Furthermore, some of the troublesome behavioral challenges, like tantrums, become fewer and farther between as she gets older. So if some glitches developed during the early years, you can now recoup and fine-tune your skills, because you know so much more about what your daughter does and does not respond to. The next couple of years in your little girl's life will be a great time to continue with your strong, conscious parenting and enjoy seeing her develop more and more.

Developmental Factors

Your daughter is now four or five years old. At the preschool age, energy abounds in little girls. They can do so many things and want to show off their skills. You are your daughter's audience, and she loves to tell you what is on her mind. As you are busy setting out the cereal bowls one morning, your little girl may be bubbling over about what will happen at preschool that day—her teacher is bringing in a kitten. As your daughter tells you all about it, you may catch your breath for a moment because you realize how well she can now speak. You notice that she can:

O Speak fluently and only has trouble with longer words. Once you correct her pronunciation, she will not forget.

O Use correct grammar in simple sentences, with only the occasional mistake. She knows her full name, address, age, at least one parent's cell phone number, and where her parents work.

O Tell you a long story about the kitten that uses more fantasy than fact and ends with her telling you what she wants for her next birthday—a puppy.

In fact, your little girl is becoming quite the conversationalist. You can almost see her brain working as she switches to yet another topic, using words that amaze you in their complexity.

She can also do so much more now. In her coloring book, she finds a picture of cats and dogs and colors them correctly. She may go outside the lines now and then, but overall she does quite a neat job. She knows all her colors and can draw pictures of many things, including a picture of you with the major body parts in place and even a face that can be recognized.

It's hard to believe, but your daughter will also start to write. In these beginning stages, she may only copy letters—mainly the easy ones such as O or V, but in no time she will tackle all of them.

When you ask your little girl to help you, she will often fly to the task. Pleasing you is at the top of her list. She may skip, dance, run, walk on tiptoes, or hop on one foot as she gets the napkins or spoons like you asked her to. When she comes home from preschool, she will dash to her room and emerge with renewed energy to play with you or her siblings.

How wonderful it is to see her be able to amuse herself. When she runs out of games to play by herself, she will listen to your suggestions and start on something else with a heartwarming eagerness.

Her Toys and Hobbies

Does your little daughter have her own library? If she does not, encourage her to set one up. Her love of books is paramount. Reading is one of the most important school skills, and the more you read to her, and she to you—mainly by retelling to you and embellishing what she remembers you having read to her previously—the more her reading readiness increases. Soon she will recognize words that recur and trace them. Her love for letters will extend beyond her tracing them on paper or trying to write her name in capitals. When you drive with her on the highway, she will begin to point to billboards and greet the large letters on them like long-lost friends.

Besides your daughter's books and music, which may consist of kids' songs or the soundtrack from a favorite movie, her toy collection will include a variety of items that reflect her special likes and hobbies. Avoiding gender stereotypes in toys can start early. Provide your daughter with a range of toys, including blocks and puzzles, which can build spatial skills, as well as dolls and stuffed animals, which can foster language in pretend play. There's no need to push one toy over another, as "boy toys" and "girl toys" are not inherently better or worse for your developing daughter. You do not have to have an entirely gender-neutral toy box either. Just don't limit your choices; having a variety of toys allows your daughter to select her own favorites.

Approve of your daughter's developing interests while guiding her toward what you feel is suitable, without stifling her unique personality. She may fall in love with the latest version of the same toys you had at her age, or she may choose the exact opposite. She may be thrilled to hold the precious baby doll you played with or the building blocks your grandparents set aside, or she may hand them back to you at once.

PRESCHOOL PROGRAMS

Of course, how and where your little girl spends her day will influence some of her toy choices and hobbies. Often what she sees at preschool—or on TV—is something she will clamor for when you are close. It is during this time that girls become exposed to popular movies, toys, and consumer goods marketed to them. Everywhere you turn, her new favorite character may be on anything from a shirt to food products at the store (who knew princesses endorsed certain brands of green beans?). She may ask for the latest Disney princess outfit and know the whole plot line even though she has never seen the movie. You will have less control over what she is exposed to, and her interests will widen dramatically. She may latch on to an interest and go deep, wanting every related toy and product, or she may flit from one thing to the next. Either way, she will be readily able to tell you her likes and dislikes.

Your awareness of media and products that send gender-stereotyped messages can help guide the choices you make for your daughter. You have the power to help her choose toys that send positive messages and promote self-esteem, compassion, and other traits and values you believe are important.

KINDERGARTEN PROGRAMS

At around age five or sometimes as late as six, many children advance from a preschool program to regular kindergarten in a public, private, or faith-based setting. Carefully read the curriculum—the listing of instructional goals—of the kindergarten program your daughter attends. Ask for an explanation of the terms you do not understand. You may find the program to be quite complex or challenging compared to the kindergarten you remember attending.

Now, much more academic pressure has been placed on the early years in a child's education, so that she will be completely ready once she enters first grade. Kindergarten offerings reflect that shift, and you will likely see her having academic work that used to be reserved for first grade. You can help your daughter with balance by fostering non-academic activities and spending time out of school helping her find what she enjoys most.

Fortunately, your daughter is now old enough to tell you what activities she thinks are fun. When you ask her what she would like to do on a free afternoon, most often she will opt for playing with her friends. There is great value in having unstructured downtime when she can play freely and make her own fun. Kids learn from free play as well as teacher- and parent-led activities. Allowing your child to be "bored" can spur her imagination and give her opportunities to be creative. Your daughter may also be interested and already participating in organized sports, activities, and hobbies. These can be great opportunities for friendship, exercise, and learning, but avoid overscheduling your kindergarten daughter with too many activities.

There is also a real danger of parents inadvertently trying to live their unmet desires through their own child. There is nothing wrong with exposing her to a variety of activities. Listen to your daughter if she begins to express resistance to the activity you were sure she would love. Introduce her to a variety of activities, but don't go overboard and push her into things that don't interest her. She will go because she wants to please you, but you don't want her to be going out of obligation to you. Be sure you listen to and honor your daughter's feelings.

Social Interactions

One thing that makes your preschool daughter happy is playing with other children. It may come as something of a surprise to you, but children have to learn how to play. If your daughter has developed a liking for one or two of her classmates or perhaps the children of your neighbors or friends, give her a chance to trot out her toys and interact with her cohorts as often as you can arrange it. She is now at an age when she needs to play with other children, so she can learn to share as well as assert herself if a peer is being too rough or not playing fair.

LANGUAGE AND PLAY

Social skills are among the many things children must learn, and if you've ever tried to encourage three- or four-year-olds to share, you know how challenging the process can be. Children must learn how to get along with others and to gain a sense of what others are feeling and thinking. The process takes time and a great deal of patience and coaching from parents.

Very young children engage in what is called parallel play; that is, they tend to sit together, each playing independently. They are in the same space, and they are playing, but they are not playing together. Eventually, a child will begin to notice other children and express curiosity about them. A little girl is likely to explore her new acquaintance by touching or poking him or by grabbing at a toy to see what he will do.

When greeting and saying goodbye to friends or family members, don't force your child to hug or kiss hello or goodbye. Allowing her to choose how she greets others, as long as it is polite and appropriate, sends the message that she is in charge of her body and what makes her feel comfortable. If she doesn't want to hug or kiss, give her an alternative such as a wave or a high-five.

Not surprisingly, social relationships tend to work out better when a child has learned to use words. It also helps when a child has acquired some emotional skills and can read faces and body language to understand whether to approach a new person. Several studies have noted that girls tend to be more collaborative in their play; they talk and make rules together about how their game will go. Boys often form groups with a leader, and the chosen activity is usually physical. There are also within-group differences, meaning some girls will be more physical and some boys will be more cooperative than others.

Your daughter will need time and opportunities to practice her social skills. Be sure you offer her opportunities to be with children her own age. When things go awry (and they inevitably will), don't punish or scold.

Instead, take time to explore with your daughter what happened, why it happened, and what she could do to get a better result next time. Parents can help with the development of social skills by coaching children with their friends, rather than intervening.

LEARNING TO SHARE

Learning to share is important because from birth on, children are self-centered and develop a strong desire to have things. Whenever they see something new, they want it, no matter how many stuffed animals they already have. Also from about age two on, they see the world in regard to personal ownership. They talk about "my" house (where your family lives), "my" car (the car you drive), and "my" swimming pool (where you take your little girl to splash in the water). To a little girl, her bed and her room and her toys matter—a lot. She sees these items in terms of herself, and the word *mine* crops up often in her conversation.

Little girls do not automatically know how to share, but they can learn quickly. Explain some basic rules to your daughter and her playmates, and use them systematically. Here are some sharing rules many parents explain to their children and their little visitors:

○ Do not grab another child's toy unless you get permission first. Ask every time you come over, and don't assume the permission lasts for more than one visit.

○ Rather than saying "no" when someone asks to play with your toys, give him hope. Say something like, "You can play with it next" or "You can play with it in five minutes" (while Mom sets the kitchen timer), or "Sure, if you let me play with your toy."

○ Treat others as you want to be treated. That goes for their possessions, too. If you break something they own, you must offer to replace it. The same goes for them.

○ Change the rules as the play situations change. The main thing is to teach respect for other children and treat them as you would like to be treated.

○ If your daughter has an extra-special toy that she knows in advance she will not want to share, you can have her put it away for the playdate so there is not a conflict.

It helps when all parents agree on the sharing rules. But even if they do not, you can always inform your little girl's friends that at your house there are rules for playing with each other, inside as well as outside. Children have to learn to take turns at the swings and when hitting a ball. But what a wonderful sight it is to see your little girl and three, four, or five other children all playing peacefully and imaginatively.

CURIOSITY AND YOUR PRESCHOOLER

During the preschool years, even the best-behaved little girl will struggle to comply with adult expectations. There's just too much going on in her world. You will be far more successful at setting limits, communicating, and getting along with your daughter when you take time to be curious about who she is becoming and what her world is like. Here are some things to ponder:

○ Preschoolers do not experience time in the same way adults do. Five minutes for you may feel like an hour for your daughter. If you expect patience, you will both be disappointed in the results.

○ Preschoolers are far more interested in the process than the product. You may want a painting to hang on your refrigerator. Your daughter may have found smearing the paint with her fingers satisfying enough and may never get around to the final product.

○ Preschoolers cannot tell fantasy from reality the way you can. If it happens on the movie screen or on television, it's "real" and no amount of debate can convince her otherwise. (This fact is a good reason to exercise caution where the media are concerned.)

○ Preschoolers love to ask questions. While the constant "whys" and "how comes" can be exhausting, questions are how little children learn. Be sure to take time to listen to your daughter.

Developmental psychologist Erik Erikson said there are two stages in children's emotional development during the preschool years. At two, they learn autonomy, which is why two-year-olds love the word *no*. At three, they begin to practice initiative, the ability to make and carry out their own plans. Both of these stages create challenges for parents. Remember that it's normal development, and it is not about you.

Curiosity about your daughter's perceptions, feelings, and ideas is always a good place to begin as you solve problems and face challenges together. Take time to express curiosity before passing judgment; it will always help you parent your daughter wisely.

Fostering Healthful Habits

In addition to play, there are other healthful habits you want to help your daughter develop. Anything that promotes her physical and mental health falls under this category, including eating right and exercising. These healthful habits can be small changes in what you already teach her, or they can be major. But nothing is wasted on your daughter, especially if you practice what you propose. If she picks up the being-active habit now, she will keep it up in the years to come.

EATING RIGHT

Another healthful habit for your little daughter is eating healthfully. Examine foods carefully before you serve them to her. Your daughter's tendency to imitate her parents comes in very handy here. If you and your spouse eat a health-conscious diet, your little girl will follow along. So make a game of shopping for groceries with her. You can give your daughter her own short grocery list (use pictures if she cannot read yet) and help her shop. Get your daughter involved in meal planning and food preparation. Children love to be invited; they usually resist being commanded. Even toddlers can rinse and tear lettuce, put cheese slices on hamburger buns, and bring napkins or silverware to the table. Your daughter is more likely to eat something she has helped prepare. Have her become savvy at an early age about what is good for her and what is not.

Even the most health-oriented household has to make allowances for someone's sweet tooth now and then. Teach her about moderation and set a good example yourself. If you are eating a cookie after every meal, she will want to as well. If you reserve cookies for special occasions, such as a birthday party, she will learn that these are treats and not staples.

HEALTHY BODY

The seeds of healthy body image are planted early and they start with you. If you make negative comments about your weight or how you look in front of your daughter, she will be listening and internalizing what she is "supposed" to look like. The media already send messages about impossible beauty standards, so keep any negative comments about your body and others' bodies out of earshot of your daughter. She may be naturally curious and ask questions about why some people are heavy and others thin. Answer honestly: Some people are bigger because their parents were bigger and some people are bigger because they don't make healthy choices about eating or exercising. Reinforce that every body is different and as a family, you are trying to make sure that you make healthy body choices.

Your preschool daughter is also ready for basic conversations about her own body and keeping safe. While it may be unpleasant to think about, the reality is that there are far too many young girls who experience unwanted touching from others. Bath time and when changing clothes are good opportunities to chat with your daughter about the importance of telling you if anyone asks her to keep a secret about her body, or touches her in a way she does not like. Teach her about her private parts and how she should not let anyone touch her or be asked to touch anyone else's private parts. Conversations about "good touch" and "bad touch" should be avoided, because she is too young to make such evaluations. Keep the focus on the message that you never keep body secrets and she will never be in trouble for telling you if someone made her uncomfortable.

Teaching Your Daughter Resilience

In addition to encouraging your little girl's development of healthful habits, you want to do your best to foster a positive and optimistic attitude.

While it is unnatural to be happy every second—after all, there are tragic and unpleasant events in everyone's life at some time—you want to instill in her a deep sense of optimism and help her develop coping skills. Teach her that she may not be able to control what happens at school or with her friends, but she can control her response to what happens.

MODELING HEALTHY COPING

Your everyday expression will imprint itself on your girl's mind and heart. In this, she is a mirror image of you, so erase your frown and try your best to smile or laugh. Giggle with your daughter, tell funny stories, and read a book of goofy jokes or riddles together. Be silly with her; she will remember and cherish these times!

When things go sour in your own day, be explicit with your daughter about how you recovered—by talking it out, engaging in mindfulness or self-soothing practices, reframing the problem as an opportunity to grow, etc. She learns how to cope from watching you, so model happiness and resiliency as often as you can. Be sure to include the following important joy components:

- **An ability to lessen stress.** Having a place for everything helps. Provide her with a bookcase and other storage space for her toys, papers, and favorite must-haves. Not being able to find her "blankie" can seriously stress out a little girl. Also teach her to soak in a warm tub, and play with her bath toys while soothing music wafts in from another room.

- **An ability to listen.** What you want to do is start talk time. Every evening after supper and right before your little girl goes to sleep, ask her about her day, and let her talk about whatever. If she isn't in a talking mood, share a moment you enjoyed with her during the day.

- **A toolkit of mindfulness activities.** Mindfulness is a powerful tool for developing focus, inner calm, and appreciation/joy. It need not be sitting cross-legged in silence and meditating with your preschooler. You can sit together and imagine a relaxing scene or listen to a guided meditation, have her "rock" a favorite stuffed animal to sleep with her deep belly breaths while lying down, blow bubbles together to practice deep breathing, or go on a mindful walk with her and have her use her senses to experience what is around her. Taking a break with her and doing only one thing, such as coloring or enjoying a snack together and focusing on the taste, can also be calming.

O **Faith and spirituality.** Some parents choose to expose their daughters to religion and religious services. Others prefer instilling a broader sense of spirituality, which can encompass things like awe, gratitude for the blessings in one's life, and being connected with others. Talking about your values with your daughter, whether religious or not, can give her a solid foundation.

With these skills, your daughter will be able to cope with life's bumps and unexpected disappointments. This process will be of great help as you guide her on to the next stage of her development—starting school.

Getting Ready for School

There is great excitement in the air as you introduce your daughter to her next adventure—being a student. For now, you want her to have the best possible start to school, and that begins with building her enthusiasm. Tell her about the thrilling time that is ahead. Mention the many new things she will learn and the many new children she will meet. Long before school starts, take her to visit "her" school.

EASE SCHOOL ANXIETY

If possible, let your daughter visit her future school at a quiet time. Let her amble along the halls, count the classroom doors, maybe even peek into the cafeteria. Now is when that talk time you have put in place will come in handy. At your next session, ask your daughter what she wants to know about her new school. Tell her what fun lessons she will experience. Next time you swing by the school, let her lead you. Does she remember where the bathrooms and the library are? Where can she go if she gets lost?

Long before the first bell rings, try to acknowledge whatever anxious thoughts she has, and take steps to assuage them. During the week before school starts, have her meet her new teacher, if possible. Some schools have official meet-and-greet opportunities, and at others you may have to e-mail first to find out if/when your daughter can come by to meet her new teacher. Reading books about transitioning to school can also be great for starting conversations about her feelings and answering any questions she might have.

Be sure that you aren't projecting your own anxiety about your little girl going to school on your daughter. Parents can also have a hard time with the transition, and this is normal! Model excitement for her, and she will also likely be excited. Showing her you are nervous about her entering the big world of school will likely make her nervous as well.

Important Points to Consider

Your preschool daughter is likely brimming with energy, enthusiasm, and curiosity. She is also ripe and ready for continued learning—both in formal school settings and out in the world in social settings. Here are a few key points you will want to keep in mind as you foster her intellect, independence, confidence, and social skills:

○ Keep a positive attitude about the transition from preschool to kindergarten and give anticipatory guidance before the transition by showing her around her new school grounds, introducing her to school staff when possible, and reading about and discussing new-school jitters with her. Provide her with messages that it is normal to be both excited and nervous at the same time, but you know she will do just fine.

O Foster your daughter's interests by giving her a range of structured and unstructured choices for her free time. Don't overdo it—one activity is probably enough.

O Just knowing about stereotypes can help you be more conscious of the choices you make in purchasing items for your daughter. Consider buying a range of toys, not just typical "girl" toys. While there is nothing wrong with traditional "girl" toys, one need not limit her interests based on gender stereotypes.

O It's never too early to talk with your daughter about healthy choices—in eating food, exercising, having a positive body image, and keeping her body safe. And don't forget to model healthy choices yourself; your daughter will learn the most from watching you.

 **CHAPTER 5**

The School Years

By the time your daughter is school-aged, you've already watched her grow and learn so much, from taking her first steps to making new friends. Her progress goes from awesome to absolutely amazing as quickly as you can blink, and you don't want to miss any of it. At this age, your daughter is still looking to you for structure and guidance, so it's important that you take advantage of your parenting opportunities. One of those opportunities occurs when your daughter enters school. While you may worry about how well your daughter will do in a school setting, and about fulfilling your own role as a conscious parent during this important time, it is best to trust your instincts as you continue to stay present with your daughter and help her grow from day to day. The progress you have observed her making so far is nothing compared to what you will see as she scrambles up the ladder from grade one to twelve. With your guidance, she may not only climb up step by step; she may also skip up the various rungs.

Getting Along with Others

To facilitate your girl's successful journey through school, prepare her before she enters first grade. First, teach her how to get along with all kinds of other children who might be her fellow travelers. That might be a little scary because there will be so many new children your daughter will meet. Many of these kids will be from her neighborhood, but some may be from other parts of town. Even in the school cafeteria, she may be assigned to a lunch table alphabetically or be asked to share a book with a child whose first language is different from her own.

No matter what type of school your daughter attends, she is in for much novelty. But what a real education this will be for your little girl. She will have a chance to meet children with a connection to various other parts of the United States or to foreign countries without ever leaving home. She will be able to mix and mingle with the offspring of all the wonderful ethnic groups that combine to make this country so great.

LEARN ABOUT OTHERS

Teach your daughter to enjoy the smorgasbord of girls and boys in her class as she sits next to them in the reading corner. When she comes home and mentions a girl or boy from a state or country different than hers, look at a map or atlas with her. Show her the place and answer her questions about it. This is what you want your girl to develop—a curiosity about people and places that interest her.

During the first few weeks of school, watch out for any changes in your daughter. If she develops a sudden dislike for school, investigate the reasons immediately. Schools will honor a parent's request for another classroom assignment, but only if the reason is valid.

Think of your daughter's school as a microcosm of the world, and think of her association with her new classmates as her chance to understand other people and cultures. This is a great opportunity for her to expand her understanding of the globe. In addition to meeting these youngsters in person, it will be fun for her to:

○ Read about children with different backgrounds

○ Meet these youngsters in person outside of school

○ Get an insight into what motivates them

Education goes far beyond book learning. It includes learning about real people, places, and things.

Besides just noticing the diversity in her classroom, your daughter gets to practice her sharing skills. Remind her to be willing to wait in line, wait her turn, and raise her hand if she wants the teacher's attention. Getting along with others is especially important in school, because an orderly classroom where rapid learning takes place cannot exist without the cooperation of all the children.

SHARE YOUR EXPERIENCES

Share with your daughter some stories about when you first went to school and had to learn everything from scratch. Tell her about some of your elementary school teachers, early assignments, and favorite books. Do you have any school mementos to show her? Show-and-tell is not just an enjoyable classroom activity; it is fun at home, too.

Designate a corner in your kitchen, den, or living room as your daughter's homework zone. Don't send her off to her room to do her homework, at least not during her first few school years. You want to be available to provide support should she get frustrated with an assignment. Be careful not to jump in too soon, though, as there is value in her grappling with concepts on her own. Ask her questions about the task and reinforce the message that learning is about making mistakes, trying your best, and seeking help when needed. Messages about the importance of effort over the ability to do things easily will give her permission to struggle a bit. Also, an encouraging word from you may lead to less dawdling. Make homework a family endeavor.

Girls and School Culture

American schools have a long and varied history. During the early years of our country, several unique factors influenced our educational system, including the existing Native American child-rearing practices, the settlers' home cultures, and an emerging sense of nationality.

Early on, the idea of practicality was most important. Therefore, much learning was gained in the school of hard work. Later, as towns and school districts began to emerge, boys in many parts of the new country received a rudimentary education, but girls were generally excluded. While this practice changed gradually, most often girls were admitted to the public schools many years after the boys. This practice had a detrimental effect on girls' scholastic achievements.

Even when school attendance for all children finally became mandatory, girls did not fare as well overall as they should have. They were often channeled into less academically rigorous classes, such as home economics. They were caught up in the enormous bureaucracy that comprises today's public schools. Like all huge bureaucracies, schools are slow to change.

What may work very well for you is your networking with other parents. Join the PTA and other supportive parent groups. As you work within those organizations, you will meet parents with girls who are doing well and enjoying school. Feel free to reach out to them for advice if your girl is struggling. Too often, parents feel they have to reinvent the wheel when all they have to do is connect with other parents who have already successfully shepherded their daughters through the school system.

DOES QUIET EQUAL GOOD?

Even today quite a few schools still show traces of the belief that boys are more deserving of an education than girls. This attitude does not show itself in pupil attendance, which is usually higher among female students than among male students, but it is seen in lowered expectations for many girls. For example, when boys show a disinterest in schoolwork, they are often the subjects of emergency meetings arranged by the school faculty. The male students' parents are notified at once and extra lessons are advised. When girls follow a similar pattern and lose interest in school, they are often allowed to slide—just as long as they behave in class. One underlying reason is that boys may tend to act out when they become disengaged in school, which disrupts the school environment.

TEACHERS AS MENTORS

It's important to remember that you, as a parent, are not working in isolation. You can present a united front that is fortified by your capable coworkers—the staff at your daughter's school—who will do all they can to facilitate your girl's swift and smooth rise to the top. Working hand in hand with your daughter's teachers, you become part of a team that is dedicated to bringing out the best in children, yours among them. What they bring to the table, you supplement, and they complement what you have already instilled in your girl. In fact, your child's teachers can mentor your daughter to such a degree that she will blossom both in and outside of school.

Why Girls Excel . . . or Fail

Girls, like all youngsters, rise to meet our expectations. When you have high hopes for your daughter, she will know it and have them, too. Likewise, when you expect less of your daughter, in all likelihood she will strive less.

Make sure you tell your daughter every so often that only the sky is the limit. Tell her how lucky she is—and you are—to enjoy so many opportunities that were missing in the past. Do not push her, but do nudge and encourage her. Begin early, before her school years start. Do not let your girl express a girl-negative attitude without setting her straight.

Mindset Matters

Carol Dweck, a psychologist from Stanford University, has pioneered interesting work on how one's mindset can affect learning. She distinguishes two mindsets: fixed and growth. In the case of the fixed mindset, a child believes (and is told by others) that her intelligence and abilities are fixed or permanent traits (e.g., "I'm smart" or "I am not a math person"). When children adopt this attitude, they are more likely to focus on their performance than on learning, take fewer risks academically for fear of what doing poorly would mean, and perform less well on tasks they perceive they are "not good at." In the growth mindset, a child believes abilities and intelligence can be improved with effort. This mindset makes children more open to taking risks (because they can work harder next time if they do poorly), persist longer and on more complex tasks, and have a healthier attitude toward failure.

Some girls adopt a fixed mindset toward a number of activities that traditionally may be considered "male" in nature, such as math, science, technology, and mechanical things. There is no evidence of any neurological benefit from being a male in these areas. Small differences, such as infant and toddler males having slightly better spatial abilities and infant and toddler females being stronger in language, are minor and not sustained over time. Gender stereotypes reinforce these small differences, causing larger gaps to form as a self-fulfilling prophecy. With your daughter, you want to insist that anyone can learn anything with effort. Emphasize that learning involves a mixture of success and failure and that very few people are naturally good at things without exerting some effort.

Use phrases that emphasize effort over ability with your daughter. Instead of "You're good at math" you can say, "You have worked so hard on your multiplication tables!" If she is struggling, you can say, "Mistakes are how you learn" and "Challenges help you grow."

Perfectionism Is Overrated

Perfectionism is the process of trying to do your best and still being displeased with the result. Perfection should never be the goal; it is not a final destination. The word comes from the Latin *perfectus* and means "finished" or "completed," but it does not have to mean "impeccable." That distinction is especially important for girls as they go through school. Too many girls latch on to the idea that whatever they do—from a social studies project to a term paper—has to be flawless. Often that quest for perfection preoccupies them to the exclusion of everything else. Or it can paralyze them and keep them from getting started on an assignment.

Therefore, teach your daughter that perfection in scholastic work is overrated. Nothing should ever be "faultless to a fault." Inform her that you expect her to make good grades, but she should not obsess over each tiny percentage point. That is why a range of numbers is assigned to each letter grade: A ranges from 90 to 100, B ranges from 80 to 89, and so on. Explain that aiming for a grade range is a good thing, but making her best effort and learning new and interesting things are more important than the grades she brings home. Tell her to do all her assignments as well as she can, ask for help if she needs it, and then put them out of her mind and go on.

If you discover that your daughter is becoming stressed about a school assignment, find out what about the assignment is giving her trouble. Did she start on it too late? Help her learn how to plan ahead and do a little of a project/studying at a time. Is she worrying about doing it "just right"? Help her understand that mistakes help her learn, and give her teacher information about areas where she might be struggling. Is she just plain exhausted? Teach her coping strategies such as taking periodic stress breaks to walk, play with her dog, or listen to music, and then help her take on the project one piece at a time so she does not get overwhelmed.

The best way to lessen the importance of perfection for your daughter is to relax your own standards a little. This is a great time to examine your own behavior. Do you worry too much about every tiny detail at work or at home? If so, schedule a session with yourself about your obsession to be perfect—and let your daughter get in on the process. Tell her to remind you when you stress out over trifles. As the old Chinese proverb says, "Tell me, I forget. Show me, I remember. Involve me, I understand."

Extracurricular Activities

The extracurricular activities at your daughter's school are so much more than opportunities for her to participate in a sport or club. They give her a chance to balance her mental training with her physical training. Plus, they give her confidence, increase her circle of friends, and offer her a chance to show leadership.

START-UP CLUBS

While the elementary school years do not provide as many choices of extracurricular activities as the middle and high school years, most schools have some clubs in art, drama, and science. Some schools also provide after-school meetings for students interested in computers or musical instruments, but the choices can be few and far between for first- through fifth-graders.

SCHOOL GROUPS

To find out about the after-school activities available to your daughter, ask the school office for a list. Read the list carefully and ask if there are some informal clubs or groups not mentioned in the listing. Some schools have a "library committee" or a "student leadership council" that meets only a few times a year to get student input. In general, see if there is an extracurricular activity at your girl's school that might interest her.

Once your daughter attends middle or high school, she will be swamped with school sports options. Then she may have to make some tough choices about which athletic teams she will join or try out for. The offerings of clubs will also be staggering. Some high school handbooks list dozens of available clubs with an amazing array of student involvement possibilities. Elementary school is a chance to explore and try out many different activities, and by the time she reaches the upper grades, your daughter may have landed on a few that she enjoys or is passionate about.

Don't assume that just because your child is growing up and enjoying structured activities she no longer needs free play. Free play is when children can process their experiences, work out frustrations, and learn social skills with their peers.

LISTEN UP!

Some girls fear being the center of attention and feel embarrassed when they find themselves in that position. So no matter what other after-school activities you investigate for her, make sure your daughter is involved in a group that fosters her stating an opinion and making decisions. Most PTAs have an auxiliary for students. Encourage your daughter to get involved in that. Whether the group raises funds or works on a school beautification project, your girl can discuss the options on the table, weigh the pros and cons, and make her opinions heard. Soon she will find herself speaking to her peers and to adults, and get used to expressing herself in public.

With your encouragement, your daughter may run for office in her grade-level class council or in the student government. Attending meetings and speaking up are life skills, not just school skills, and have huge benefits. Participating in these ways will make her feel secure, needed, and honored, and can lead to her becoming a very productive and involved citizen.

There are a number of wonderful organizations for young girls to get involved in that foster development of confidence, courage, leadership, friendship skills, and connectedness with community. Research local chapters of Brownies/Girl Scouts, Girls Inc., Girls on the Run, and other positive groups for girls.

Important Points to Consider

The elementary school years are full of wonderful conscious parenting opportunities. As her social and school worlds expand exponentially, keep these points in mind:

O Take an interest in your child's homework and help her when she asks. Be sure not to get too involved, though, as this will deprive her of the opportunity to develop independent learning skills and grapple with new concepts. She will develop confidence as she learns not to give up on difficult tasks.

O Seek help if you see your daughter struggling and becoming too frustrated with her work. Consult with your child's teacher and other parents for ideas about how to support her.

O Be aware that your daughter's academic performance and attitude about learning can be shaped by her mindset. Take care to emphasize a growth mindset (learning takes effort, and mistakes are how your learn) over a fixed mindset (people are naturally good at tasks, and you are either good or bad at things).

O Help your daughter find a balance between fun extracurricular activities and free playtime with her friends. Play is still of paramount importance in an elementary student's life.

 **CHAPTER 6**

Education and Achievement

There is no better way to prepare your daughter for the challenges her lifetime may bring than to provide her with an excellent education. It will serve as her admission ticket to a fulfilling and financially rewarding career. To give her a special boost in this area, help her get excited over her academic achievement, and give her every early advantage you can. Your job as a conscious parent is not to mold her into a perfect super student, but rather to build her love of learning. While clearly grades and achievement matter, cultivating a positive learning experience for your daughter is equally paramount. What's the point of being a straight-A student if she hates school every step of the way?

Building Excitement for Learning

Think of your daughter's future in increments of five years. Envision her proceeding through her school years—at five, ten, fifteen, and twenty years of age—so smoothly that she will excel in many subjects, gain knowledge to the best of her ability, and enjoy the whole process. That is your underlying goal: to help her soar in scholastics and develop her character, while enjoying the process along the way. To achieve your goal, you must be willing to provide her with every opportunity possible.

CHARACTER COUNTS

Being a person with positive character traits such as kindness, persistence, honesty, and humility is just as important as academic success. For that reason, teach your daughter about it constantly and stress its significance. Every time you notice her showing signs of inner strength and integrity, praise your girl. Model for her the traits you want her to possess—be honest and authentic with her, make positive comments about others, and show her that sticking with something, even if it is frustrating, can pay off.

If school was a struggle for you, or you did not particularly enjoy school, be careful not to let your negative feelings inadvertently trickle down to your daughter. If you describe homework or studying as an obligation she has to fulfill, rather than an activity that could inspire new learning, she will begin to internalize your perception of homework or studying as a drag. You need not be inauthentic and pretend you loved it; you can share with her that homework was not your favorite task. But you can likely find something interesting and meaningful in her work to enjoy with her.

Having a good character does not automatically equal future academic and career success, though it does help. It is also important for her as she goes through life, and if and when she has her own family. But even the strongest value system should be enhanced by strong school skills. When children feel successful at school, where they spend most of their time, they develop confidence and a sense of pride. Having a combination of strong character and confidence in academics provides a solid foundation for your daughter. There are many things you can do to promote a positive attitude toward learning and inspire natural curiosity in your daughter.

LEARNING THROUGH TECHNOLOGY

These days, even toddlers know that phones and computers hold "the answers" to questions—your daughter may love to ask questions to the automated system on your phone. Finding your child's inquisitive searches in your browser history (such as "Why is the sun so hot?" or "What makes the sky blue?") can provide a window into her curious mind. When your daughter asks questions about how things work in the world, you have a chance to teach her about using the Internet and finding reputable sources for information. Being a digital native, she may even teach you a thing or two about new sites or apps she has learned about in school or from her friends.

There are a number of excellent resources for finding high-quality apps and websites to enhance learning. Common Sense Media is an organization that provides reviews of movies, books, TV shows, and digital media that are engaging and educational. Check out www.commonsensemedia.org for a list of resources sorted by age and topic.

A HOME LIBRARY

To foster a love of learning, make it fun by stocking your home with books that can help you expand your girl's vocabulary and worldview. Invest in these three books and set them on a table in your den, living room, or kitchen—wherever you and your daughter spend the most time:

○ A dictionary (a picture dictionary if your child is younger or, if she is older, an unabridged—that is, not condensed—dictionary recommended for students of high school age)

○ An atlas of the United States and the world, plus a globe if space permits

○ A thesaurus (a book containing synonyms, words with similar meanings; and antonyms, words with opposite meanings)

Use these books like board games and have your daughter delve into them several times a week. When someone in your family comes across a new word in a book, online, or in conversation, look up the definition together. You can even highlight words you have looked up so you can begin to see how many new words you have learned together. Modeling enthusiasm for learning new words will help her enjoy learning them.

After that, play Word Treasure Hunt. Mention a simple word like *go*, and ask your girl to list all the words that have the same meaning, such as *move, drift, flow, travel*, and *sashay*. Then look in the thesaurus with her to see if she missed anything. Soon she will return the favor and laugh when you have to scramble for words that escape you. The excitement that builds with each little academic activity will be contagious.

Another great option is to play Home Travel Channel with your daughter. Every time she hears a city or country mentioned anywhere, ask her to find it in the atlas or on the globe. There are a number of interactive globes as well, which can provide fun facts about the locations you touch.

THE LIBRARY AS HOME

From the time you start reading to your daughter, take her with you to the public library, so that by the time she is three or four, she will feel at home there. Help her discover a quiet corner that she can call her nook and will gravitate to as if it were in her own home.

Once your daughter feels welcome at the public library or a "commercial" one—otherwise known as a bookstore—she can settle in and flip through the pages of a children's book. Later she will scan several chapter books by a favorite author before settling on one to read immediately and saving the others for later. As soon as your girl is old enough, make sure she gets her own library card.

At home, help your daughter organize her growing book collection, according to her own system. The more she bonds with her books, the more excited she will be to read voraciously. You want your daughter to have every advantage possible.

FUN WITH NUMBERS

At home, numbers abound! Money, time, and measurements are three major everyday applications for math. Here are some tips for building your daughter's enthusiasm about numbers:

○ Start when she is young by teaching her how much bills and coins are worth. As she gets older, help her save and budget toward an achievable goal. Help her calculate what she has, what she needs, and how much a desired item or event costs.

○ Keep an analog clock in your home and reference it. Teach her what each of the hands mean and how to tell time—first to the hour, then half, then quarter, and then minute.

○ Measuring can be super fun if she has a project she is interested in doing with you or your spouse. Measure things when she wants to rearrange her room, have her help put together furniture items with you, or have her help you design a home renovation project.

ALLEVIATE SCHOOL FEARS

Just as you familiarize your daughter with the library, do the same with her school, so that she is ready to learn without being scared, which could limit her capacity for absorbing new knowledge. These fears center on:

○ Not knowing any other children

○ Forgetting her books or locker combination

○ Getting lost in a much larger building

Even elementary schools vary greatly in size, and middle schools are often two or three times the size of an elementary school. High schools top that in size. So ask your girl what fears, if any, she might have and then ease them. Only then can the academic excitement you have created in your daughter at home continue at school. It should also permeate the way she tackles the assignments she receives as homework.

Help with Homework

Homework is an extension of work your daughter does in class and can be an overnight academic exercise or a major project that will take her a week or several to complete. But no matter how involved or lengthy, homework allows your girl to develop a better understanding of the topic at hand or to explore it further. Through a deeper immersion in any subject, she can experience the fun of learning and discover her academic strengths, especially if you help her.

Here are some tips for helping your daughter achieve homework success:

- Turn off the TV and other technological distractions (such as phones, tablets, and other technology not being used for homework).
- Provide your daughter with a "homework haven."
- Pass on your best study skills to her.

Turning off the TV during homework time stops the distractions that might interfere with your girl's learning. No matter how much she pleads her case by pointing out the volume is on low or the program is "educational," stress to her that any disruption can negatively affect the way she learns.

SINGLE-TASKING IS KEY
Multitasking while studying degrades learning. According to Russell A. Poldrack, a psychology professor at the University of California, Los

Angeles, "even if you can learn while distracted, it changes how you learn to make it less efficient and useful." Therefore, explain to your girl that watching TV will drag out her homework, whereas with the TV off, she will zip right through it.

Older students will want to have their phones or computers with them during studying. Teaching your daughter to use technology for schoolwork and not leisure activities such as using social media, watching videos, and texting or messaging with others is essential. Help her develop a system, such as having her phone on Airplane Mode for 30 minutes at a time and then using it for a 10-minute break, or disabling certain websites and features for a period of time (check out apps such as Anti-Social, SelfControl, and Freedom to start). Collaborate with her, rather than impose this on her, and you will have more success.

HOMEWORK HAVEN

Any corner in your house can be designated as the homework haven. Many parents set up a small desk in the kitchen while their children are young, so they can get started on their work—doing math—while their parents get started on theirs—fixing dinner. When your girl reaches middle or high school, she will likely be self-disciplined enough to follow her homework routine by herself in the den or her room. But for the beginning learner, doing her paperwork under Mom's or Dad's supervision is a big plus. Weaving your daughter's vocabulary words into your conversation or reciting the multiplication tables or the names of the fifty states with her, while tossing the salad, shows her how much her parents care about her homework.

STUDY SMARTS

When it comes to the efficient completion of homework assignments, you are a walking fountain of knowledge for your daughter. Since you finished your formal schooling, you are the expert on homework hints. Pass them down to your daughter while she starts her book report or does her social studies worksheet.

When your girl is finished with her homework, review it with her. Encourage her to check her work. If you find an error, see if she can spot it and self-correct it. Continue to send the message that mistakes are how one learns, so she does not view correction as criticism or your desire for perfection.

Help your daughter with her homework by assisting her in gathering materials and brainstorming with her for project ideas. Do *not* do her homework for her or give too much help. By doing so, you will deprive the teacher of needed feedback about which concepts your daughter may need retaught or reinforced.

TESTING 1, 2, 3

Another part of doing homework is getting ready for a test. To prepare your daughter for it, give her a practice quiz the day before the real one. Teach her to study short sections of her work long before a big test. Studying and reading ahead in a textbook should become part of her homework routine so that she is not overwhelmed on the day before a major exam. A calendar posted prominently in your home should list your daughter's big tests far in advance, so she can prepare herself. To be up on these dates, you want to establish good lines of communication with her teachers from the moment she steps into their classrooms.

FOSTERING NON-SCHOOL INTERESTS

Your daughter is more likely to thrive in the school environment if she also has an extracurricular activity to provide some balance. Some families have a long-standing tradition of producing girls who excel in athletic or artistic pursuits. If you are part of that type of family, it is only natural that you expect your daughter to show an ability and penchant for those activities as well. At the same time, be careful not to try to live your life through your child. She may not be a "chip off the old block" in terms of the interests you or your spouse had. She is her own person, and respecting her interests and choices will prevent conflicts and future resentments.

Connecting with Teachers and Coaches

Being a teacher, coach, or other school staff member is difficult these days. Not only is it challenging to have twenty-five or more students or budding athletes to instruct simultaneously, but the challenges of modern parenting and making ends meet have made some parents less readily available to be involved. Many parents also have less respect for the public school system than in the past. Dwindling resources and overcrowding in public schools complicate matters.

Additionally, our changing population, constantly fluctuating society, and rising expectations for school accountability have placed extra stress on educators. Although your job as a conscious parent includes being involved in your daughter's school experience, be careful not to add more pressure to her teachers' already tough jobs. Instead, communicate with the staff at your daughter's school in an efficient, helpful, and friendly manner that honors them for the hard work they do.

TEACHER NOTES

As soon as possible, establish a way of getting in touch with your daughter's teachers, according to their preference. At the school open house, find out how they want to be contacted. Some teachers prefer old-fashioned written notes sent via your daughter. Others want to be called in the evening during a specific hour, and still others want to be e-mailed or texted anytime, day or night. Once you know how to contact your girl's teachers, do not overuse their permission to contact them about every small item. Ralph Ellison said, "Education is all a matter of building bridges." Do not destroy them, or your daughter will feel the effect.

VOLUNTEER AT YOUR DAUGHTER'S SCHOOL

To connect better with the teachers who have such a huge influence on your girl's success, volunteer in their classrooms. Most elementary and middle schools ask parents or caregivers to help with special events or activities. Step up and volunteer, if your work schedule allows. Offer your assistance with updating the bulletin board or with research on a topic. Collect magazines for your girl and her classmates to use as supplemental materials, or serve as one of the judges in the science fair, even if your daughter is not participating. Find out what addition to the classroom would make the teacher's job easier, and then supply it. If your time is limited during the day, you can ask your child's teacher if there are any other tasks you can help with, such as organizing events, fundraising, or gathering needed supplies for classroom activities.

Be sure to ask your daughter what she wants you to volunteer for at her school. She will tell you. If you plan to visit her class, ask her beforehand if she wants you to speak to her in front of her classmates or just wave. Younger children will delight in your presence, and older children may want you to stay behind the scenes. Remember, the school is your daughter's second home. She knows the rules there best.

HONOR TEACHERS

When you see up close just how much teachers do every day, you will want to recognize them for their special dedication. Sit down with your daughter and discuss her teacher's hard work, his patience, and the positive influence he has not only on your daughter but also on the kids in his room, and maybe even the young teacher next door. Then decide together how you and your daughter can honor her teacher and his coworkers, all of whom are your parenting allies.

After-School Tutoring

No two students learn at the same rate. Even if your older child—or you—breezed through a certain class, your daughter may have trouble with it or say she does not like it, which is a sure indication that she will not do her best in this subject. What a perfect opportunity this is for you to investigate what is going on, and then come up with a solution, which may be after-school tutoring. Additionally, while you may want to be the answer to all of your daughter's academic struggles, it can sometimes be more important for her to receive help from someone outside her home, like a tutor. Part of conscious parenting is having the awareness to step back and ask for help when needed. This doesn't mean you aren't capable of helping your daughter; it means you are smart enough to look for outside resources.

TUTOR TIME

If your daughter brings home an unexpectedly low grade, or one that she is not satisfied with, begin by talking to her about it and dedicating some extra time to the subject. Sometimes just a little more time spent on a subject can raise the score. Also encourage her to ask her teacher for a retest, more practice sheets and homework, or an extra-credit project. Teachers enjoy seeing students take the initiative to learn more about a topic, and often will provide an alternate textbook, quizzes from a previous year, or a chance to come in at lunch and redo a unit of work that was bungled.

If you still feel that more action is needed, have a conference with your daughter's teachers to discuss other options, such as hiring a tutor. Most schools have a list of tutors they recommend.

After-school tutoring can be remedial or enriching, and should be used early as an intervention, after an educational evaluation has taken place. If, for example, your girl has missed acquiring some early grade basics, they need to be dealt with first before she can really advance.

The hours from three to six have been dubbed the "danger hours" for kids, meaning that this is the time period when kids most often get into trouble. The reason is that these are the hours when most school programs are over while many parents are still at work. Make sure your daughter has regularly scheduled activities for that time span if she is not with you or another caregiver.

TUTOR TYPES

Tutors are like teachers in that they have specialties. Some will work with your girl according to subject, such as reading or writing. Others focus on teaching study skills and getting your daughter organized. Still others can test for or identify learning disabilities, such as attention deficit hyeractivity disorder (ADHD) and dyslexia, or help ease the transition from one grade level to another.

You will find tutors who can teach foreign languages or English as a second language (ESL), prepare your daughter for advanced placement (AP) classes, or assist you if you home-school your girl or if she is homebound due to an illness. They can also be your best supporters in revving up your daughter's skills in the two school subjects that matter tremendously for girls but are too often neglected.

Math and Science Matter

For many years, society has expected boys to excel in the "harder" classes (science and math) and girls in the "easier" ones (language and social studies). The fact is all areas of study can be hard or easy, depending on the individual child and her attitude. College graduates with a math or science background usually find better-paying jobs and in more abundance. Women applicants equipped with advanced math or science skills—especially in computer science—can often write their own tickets.

One of the best ways for conscious parents to help set up their daughters for success is to lay the foundation for their girls to be math- and science-ready. It all starts with you, the parent. Yet no matter how gung-ho you are about math and science, begin with what your daughter likes. It does no good to cram those subjects down her throat when she loves literature or history. This is about *her* life and *her* gifts. As a conscious parent, it's important to step back and listen to your daughter's academic interests.

ENCOURAGING INTEREST IN MATH AND SCIENCE

Any time your daughter says something negative about science or math, counter it immediately with a positive statement. If she says, "I'm just not good in science and math," say, "Nobody knows how good they are in anything unless they try. Let me help you."

Then choose a deliberate course of action that may include the following plans:

- Encourage her to join her school's math or science club. Often this works best if she and a friend sign up together.

- Visit science museums together, and start when she is young.

- Keep an eye out for extracurricular activities infused with math, science, or technology.

- Keep books about science- and math-related careers in your home library.

- Provide her with a role model, a "cool" mathematician or scientist who can mentor her.

Computer coding classes are now offered in cities across the country. Girls Who Code is an example of an organization striving to close the gender gap in technology and foster interest in computer science. Visit www.girlswhocode.com for more information.

Great Grades Grow Great Careers

What do you want your daughter to get out of her schooling the most? If you are like many parents, the answer is to secure a good career. Consider your girl's first few years of school as skill builders. They form the building blocks of her future success in the workplace. Make sure she has been instructed well in the basics. It's no good to have her lacking in the prerequisites for the more rigorous courses. And while grades aren't the only metric for success, the reality is that good grades often reflect a combination of effort and mastering the content, which is a metric that employers and colleges take into great consideration.

It's also important to never allow your daughter to get overscheduled. As a conscious parent, you are your daughter's best advocate. Check her school schedule to see that she has a few easier courses. No girl can be in a pressure-cooker atmosphere all the time without blowing her top. One or two or three afternoons a week must be her own. You don't want your girl to burn out by the time she is sixteen.

Be sure to have your daughter start early in exploring possible career paths, but keep in mind that interests change and she should enjoy the process. Encourage her to challenge herself so she does not limit her options for higher education, but also be respectful of her own unique path. Whether she combines raising her family with a career, works intermittently outside the home, or forges ahead with a great discovery or a cure for a dreadful disease, you will be there supporting that wonderful path. The quest and love for knowledge that you instilled in your daughter will have many increasing returns.

Important Points to Consider

Your attitude toward your daughter's education can help her continue in the right direction for years to come. Consider the following:

- O Hold high expectations for your daughter's academic achievement. Emphasize that you know she will do her personal best at school and you will be there to support her every step of the way.

- O At the same time, emphasize that learning is fun, and that while grades are important, they are not the only measure you are interested in. Cultivate a love of the learning process at home. Model curiosity and join her in her quest for knowledge. She will follow your lead, especially when you start young.

- O Keep your daughter's career options wide open by encouraging her to take a variety of courses and explore a range of extracurricular activities. Women are underrepresented in science, technology, engineering, and math (STEM) careers, and fostering her interests in these areas may lead to a happy and successful future.

O Most importantly, though, it is not about pushing her into a career/interest area that she does not enjoy. Just don't limit her choices based on preconceived notions of what she may or may not like (or based on her ideas of what she may or may not be "good" at). Keep her options and her mind open!

CHAPTER 7

Peer Relationships

Your daughter's peers are very important to her. She wants to have a sense of belonging and importance and fit in with her classmates. To become an independent adult—in the not-too-distant future—she is supposed to transfer her allegiance from her parents to her peers, a process that can take years. That is the desired development in your daughter and you welcome it. But what if her peers are a bad influence on her and get in the way of her progress? Your job as a conscious parent is to allow her to build her own relationships but also be present enough in her social life to see warning signs of negative peer influence.

The Mean-Girls Phenomenon

Since the early 1980s, there has been a sharp rise in violence among boys that has not abated. While the nation's attention has been focused more on them—especially since the Columbine tragedy—attention should also be given to a more recently studied phenomenon in girls: relational aggression. Psychologists Nicki R. Crick and Jennifer K. Grotpeter define relational aggression as "harming others through purposeful manipulation and damage of their peer relationships." In plain language, it's mean-girl behavior: gossiping, spreading rumors, excluding others, and bullying (both online and in person, but more frequently online). This behavior often goes unnoticed by adults, as opposed to physical aggression that is easily observed.

Parents can educate themselves on the signs of relational aggression and ways to combat the negative effects. The Ophelia Project is a great place to start (www.opheliaproject.org), as are books like *Queen Bees and Wannabes* by Rosalind Wiseman and *Odd Girl Out* by Rachel Simmons.

You cannot protect your girl from every instance of hurt feelings, and that is not your purpose as a conscious parent. Being exposed to some peer meanness and overcoming it is emotionally healthy for her, just as is having her immune system—her body's defense department—strengthened by exposure to some germs. It is much better for your daughter to face unkindness from other girls and learn to overcome it than be shielded from it entirely and never have a chance to develop the necessary tools to combat it successfully. Without experiencing that struggle, your daughter would be deprived of the confidence that is a by-product of overcoming acts of rudeness and hostility by her classmates.

MEAN-GIRLS CONDUCT

Although you cannot protect your daughter from every instance of mean behavior by her peers, you can arm her with knowledge about what to expect from some not-so-nice girls in her world and how to be prepared for it. Then she can disarm and defuse any of her classmates or "friends" who might want to mistreat her. This mistreatment can take the forms of other girls engaging in:

1. Stealing her friends

2. Excluding her from social events

3. Stabbing her in the back (figuratively)

4. Spreading lies and rumors about her

5. Posting disparaging things about her online

6. "Catfishing" her (making a fake profile and pretending to be someone else online in order to fool or confuse her)

Know your daughter's moods, and do not feel complacent if your daughter doesn't report outright physical abuse, such as pushing, punching, or shoving, from female classmates. Girls usually express their anger toward other girls in subtler ways, such as through mean-spirited notes, phone calls, instant messages or text messages, and other electronic communications in a powerful peer rumor mill that aims to inflict pain.

There are many other ways girls can be mean to one another, but if your daughter is aware of the most prevalent signs of hostility some girls in her circle may exhibit, she can easily dodge or deflect them. Also, realizing that it is not the girls themselves—only their unkind behaviors—that she should object to, your girl can watch out for any red flags shown by other girls and avoid the accompanying negatives.

The first piece of information to give your daughter is to let her know what types of mean girls, identified here by their behavior, she may run across in her school, neighborhood, or community. Here are some steps you can take:

O Teach her to recognize the kinds of unfriendly or aggressive girl behaviors that exist. Mean-girls behavior can come from your daughter's very own friend circle.

O Stress to her that it's important that she learn to deal with girls showing those characteristics, but only on her terms and conditions.

O Reinforce the message that the stronger and more confident she is in her own self-worth, the less likely she is to be a target for a mean girl. Teach assertiveness (the website http://doingrightbyourkids.com is a great place to start for ideas).

O Advise her to avoid them and help her friends avoid them as well, if the mean girls resist her assertiveness and attempts to communicate with them in a positive way.

O Be a resource for your child, but don't swoop in to rescue her every time a girl is mean to her. Help her problem-solve ways to deal with the behavior and let her gain some chops in getting past rude comments and hurtful behavior.

O Nip any mean-girl behavior you see or hear about from your child in the bud. If she is the one excluding or gossiping about another girl, teach empathy for the other girl's feelings.

Watch how you treat women. If you are nice to their faces but criticize them and make disparaging remarks about them to others, you are teaching your daughter to become a hypocritical and backstabbing girl who will become a backstabbing young woman.

MEAN-GIRL TYPES

Parents must not forget that all the unfriendly or hostile girls your daughter meets have their reasons for the way they behave. Most often these reasons arise from their home life, from the way they were raised, or from what they have observed in their parents' relationships. For example, if they see their parents manipulate their friends, they may become manipulators. Or if their parents live to gossip about their neighbors, their daughters will become gossipers, too.

Yet no matter how adept some girls become in their negative machinations regarding others, they rarely feel good about themselves. In truth, most of them feel miserable and—by lashing out at your daughter and her friends, most often verbally—they want to make other girls feel miserable, too. Based purely on their behavior, these mean girls can be divided into the following categories:

1. **Snobs.** These girls judge the world, your daughter, and other girls only in terms of their "wealth" or their connection, if any, to famous people.

2. **Gossips.** These girls love to spread around bits of information, especially if it is negative, and they tend to embellish.

3. **Teasers.** These girls enjoy finding a weakness or sore spot in other girls, including your daughter, and needling them about it constantly in a mean way.

4. **Bullies.** These girls, though rarer than the others, threaten to, or actually do, physically hurt other girls.

5. **Traitors.** These girls can be psychologically dangerous in the long run. They will gain your daughter's complete confidence and then betray her by word or deed. Therefore, they can leave lasting scars.

6. **Cyber Frenemies.** These girls act sweet in person while unleashing their meanness on the Internet. They pretend to be friends while— via texting, e-mailing, or posting on social media—they are cowardly enemies who want to bring your daughter down.

7. **Cyber Pit Bullies.** These girls, though rare, set out to inflict as much harm as possible. They are extremely cyber savvy and their hobby is spreading vicious rumors about other girls, infiltrating their e-mail accounts, "spamming" or sending viruses, and so forth, even after they have been warned off.

The combination of a few of those mean-girl types, along with a bad school atmosphere, can lead to tragic results.

Always keep in mind that no girl is born mean; she becomes that way. An unkind girl is the product of her environment, just as your daughter is the product of hers. Sad to say, but some girls come from homes where snobbishness, gossiping, sarcastic teasing, bullying, and betrayal—in real life or in the digital domain—go on every day. These patterns of behavior are taught to them and condoned not only by their parents but also by their siblings.

For that reason, you want your daughter to understand that planned acts of unkindness from other girls are rooted in their personal background, but that does not excuse their behavior. Rather than respond in kind, she should pity girls whose character training has been neglected.

MEAN-GIRL TACTICS

In case some types of mean girls target your daughter, she needs to know how to handle them and defend herself. It is always best to assume that at some point in her school career she will be exposed to rude remarks or other signs of relational aggression by other girls. Therefore, a generic approach to run-of-the-mill bad acts, such as contemptuous glares, expressions of disgust, or abrupt turning away, can come in handy. Here are a few tactics your daughter can use:

O Try not to take the meanness personally. Focus on what she *can* control—not the mean behavior but her reaction to it.

O Try to feel sorry for the girl who acts that way.

O Never revert to the same behavior herself.

O Try to take the upper hand by saying, "Sorry, I didn't realize you are having a bad day."

Also, practice with your daughter how to stand in a powerful way, facing her detractors with her spine straight and her head up. Tell her she can send any mean girls scurrying with her stance, attitude, and confident signals. One thing to remember about mean-acting girls is that they usually look for the meekest and quietest girl in the crowd and leave stronger girls alone. To take charge in a negative situation is to be empowered. Empower your girl not to be a doormat. Instead, rehearse with her how to take a stand against unkind girls.

You also want to make sure your daughter has some classmates who will insulate her against being singled out and give her a network for support and for venting her frustrations.

LONG-TERM ADVANTAGES

The heartwarming part of teaching your daughter about dealing with mean girls is that you are giving her another important life skill. In the years to come, she may run into some unfriendly girls in various mutations in college, on the job, in her neighborhood, in her house of worship, or at her workout place—as her superiors, coworkers, or subordinates. There is always a chance your girl will run across an unhappy woman or two who try to make others feel as bad as they do via their mean-spirited tendencies.

COUNTER MEANNESS

With her insight into mean girls, your daughter will know how to handle their behavior. She will recognize any spiteful females from a mile away. That does not mean your girl will not feel a twinge of hurt when confronted by female rudeness, but the twinge will be just another sign that she is making progress. Physical exercise can make her sore. Exercising her relationship muscles is no different. Your daughter will get better each time she triumphs over the disrespect from other girls. Plus, being empowered, she will be able to help other girls who contribute to her growth and make her life more fun.

Finding Positive Friends

One of the best protective strategies you can help teach your daughter is to surround herself with numerous positive friends. You cannot be with her in school, after school, and during her practices and meetings. You cannot sift through her classmates and kick the negative ones to the curb, but you can give your daughter every opportunity to associate with positive friends who add to her well-being rather than subtract from it.

Girls change in their stages of forming friendships as they go through their school years. Typically, your daughter and her friends graduate from an early stage of side-by-side playing to interacting as they play. Next, they move to friendships in groups and the best-friend stage. After that, girls reach the clique stage, the interest-based group stage, and finally—toward the end of high school—they develop an accepting spirit and openness to finding friends almost anywhere.

It is important to remember that not all girls follow the friendship stages exactly. Some linger at a certain stage, while others skip one or two. No matter where your daughter finds herself in the development of friends as she gets older, she can benefit from having a wide range of peers to choose from. Should her friends move, for example, or should she change schools, she will be able to select new or more friends with ease and confidence.

BENEFITS OF GIRLFRIENDS

According to Lyn Mikel Brown, a women's studies and education scholar, girls make use of their girlfriends as their "emotional and psychological safety nets." With their friends beside them, they will be braver, speak out more often on important topics, and show more courage as they stand up for others—and for themselves.

Therefore, having girlfriends is most important for your daughter. She needs them as her allies and to make her feel strong, respected, and successful. Your daughter may already have one fabulous friend or best buddy, but how can you make sure that her army of allies expands?

TYPES OF GIRLFRIENDS

Explain to your daughter that girlfriends come in many different forms, from casual to close ones, and that it is best to have at least one in each group. Life for a growing girl is filled with possibilities, so she should not limit herself to just one relationship with one girl. She should be sure her circle includes many different girls. Here are a few types of good friends:

○ **Study buddies.** These girls are in her classes; they are motivated and, like your daughter, want to excel in scholastics.

○ **Good friends.** These are girls your daughter is comfortable with; they make her life more fun. They can be old friends she reconnects with, or new friends she meets now.

○ **Best buds.** This is usually one girl, or two, who is a close, reliable, and unwavering friend she can talk to about everything.

○ **Soul pals.** These are girls with whom your daughter can form a forever friendship because they think and feel alike, almost like twins. No matter how much they grow and change, their connection stays the same.

Assuming your daughter is ready to make more friends, point out places where she can best find some, such as clubs, extracurricular activities, or community groups.

DEMONSTRATING GOOD FRIENDSHIPS

By watching you, your daughter has already learned the friendship basics. But it will not hurt for you to remind her of the most important friend-keeping strategies:

1. Being trustworthy and not telling her friends' secrets unless they are in danger or need help

2. Not being envious or jealous, and remaining good friends even when the going gets tough

3. Sharing some of her failures, as well as her successes, to bond better

You, the parent, have a lot of influence on your daughter's friend-making skills. You can make your house a place where your girl and her friends want to hang out by providing plenty of healthy drinks and snacks and appropriate movies. You can encourage her to bring her girlfriends home, but do not critique them harshly.

The more you find fault with your daughter's friends, the more she might feel she has to defend them. The same goes for the groups you may find your daughter beginning to cultivate. Forbidding her to associate with certain peers may cause your daughter to find them more appealing. Instead, focus on helping your daughter understand how her friends make her feel. Eventually, she will realize that there are girls who build her up and those who try to tear her down.

You can also be a good listener when your girl complains about her friends or about being excluded from something they do. Listen to her with all your attention and tell her that her friendship dilemmas will diminish as she gets older.

Tricky Cliques

A clique is a close group of friends that outsiders see as exclusionary. Cliques exist in most schools from middle school up and can be either "iron cliques"—permanent ones—or more casual ones that last only a short time.

As girls move to more independence and individuation—the process of becoming a separate and distinct identity—they tend to miss the stability of the close-knit family unit that once was the center of their lives. As a result, they look for a family substitute and form groups or cliques.

Overall, group behavior is important because from middle school on the conduct of the group your girl associates with has an enormous impact on her. Surrounding herself with girls who look or act similarly makes her separation from her mother and father easier. For that reason, joining a clique is a positive developmental step, but cliques can be tricky.

Some cliques can be very beneficial, but when a clique is toxic, trouble can start. How can you know? Ask yourself what the purpose of the clique is. Why are the members hanging out together? If it is for a school-connected or other positive purpose, such as a sport, that is one thing. But some cliques have no purpose other than gossiping about and excluding other girls. So if the clique meets only to denigrate others, help your daughter to find a more positive group. You do not want her to be pulled into doing something hurtful by peer pressure, also known as the "clique squeeze." Not having a group to belong to is much better for your girl than associating with a clique that could hurt her in some way.

One of the best ways to instill consciousness in your daughter is to discourage her from always affixing a judgmental label, such as "preppie," "nerd," "jock," "goth," or "loser," to every girl she sees, based only on superficial evidence. Encourage her to look beneath the surface. Too many girls write off others according to their clothes, hairstyle, weight, or accent.

Warn your daughter about girls who live only for texting and posting things about themselves on social media. Encourage her to be friends (in person and online) with girls who are not self-obsessed and don't use technology as a tool for mean behavior. Similarly, encourage your daughter to post more than just selfies on her own pages and feeds, and teach her how to be judicious about what to post about herself and others.

Unsafe Friends

Countless proverbs warn of the strong influence your daughter's friends can have on her, such as "Show me your friends and I'll tell you who you are." While you do not want to belittle your daughter's friends, you do want to notice their appearance and the way they act, especially how they conduct themselves when they think you cannot see them. It is important to keep your comments about her friends you don't approve of observational in tone, so that your daughter does not get defensive of her friend choices.

SHARE YOUR WIDSOM

If your daughter is gravitating toward friends who make you uneasy, talk to her about what you have observed about them. Take care not to out-right criticize your daughter's friends, but rather check in with her about how they make her feel. Share your wisdom and offer anecdotes from your own friendships. For example, if her friend says unkind things about others, there is a good chance this friend is also saying unkind things about your daughter. If her friend is engaging in risqué behavior, such as sexting or dressing in an overly provocative way for her age, now is the time to talk about healthy expressions of sexuality.

When your daughter is younger, you have some control over whom she spends time with. When she is older, you will have to help your daughter evaluate her friends and make good friend choices. You cannot shield her from friends who you do not like, but you can teach her what a good friend is and how to extract herself from an unhealthy friendship.

FRIEND CHOICES

You may find that your daughter gravitates toward girls with problematic backgrounds because she is kindhearted and wants to help girls in need. While this is something to be commended, you should also teach her that she cannot singlehandedly solve other girls' problems at this stage of her life. Help her navigate the line between being supportive and being overinvolved at the expense of her own emotional energy.

Encourage her to make friends everywhere—at school, at athletic practices, in the neighborhood, and at community activities. Cast a wide net and she will have more friends to fall back on if a friendship goes sour. Having friends from all social spectrums and ethnicities can be a big plus for your daughter. The more she widens her circle, the more she can learn from all kinds of talented girls.

Brand-Name Pressures

Sometimes girls are drawn into groups that have shallow values. To the members of this type of clique, only a girl's outer wrappings matter. Designer labels and complicated, expensive hair routines rule, not what is inside a girl. When you find your daughter suddenly trying to fit in with an extremely high-maintenance group, give her a wake-up call. Tell her that trying to fit in with girls who cherish designer purses more than people may make her more popular, but that the word *popular* means average or ordinary. She should not strive so hard to be just ordinary. She should strive to be extraordinary.

If you find your daughter refuses to wear anything that does not have an expensive brand name, ask her to use her own money to buy brand-name apparel. You will buy her what is attractive yet reasonable. If she still insists on the designer shirt, point her in the direction of some part-time work opportunities where she can earn extra cash.

Bullying: Victim or Victimizer?

In recent years, bullying has received a lot of attention. In fact, about 22 percent of all students have been bullied in ways that go beyond the occasional teasing or name calling. While girl bullies are much rarer than boy bullies, they do exist. Usually they do not use their fists. Instead, they use safety pins to "accidentally" stab other girls, they trip or elbow them, or they knock their books off the desk. These days, girls bullying via text and online is also common.

Watch for these classic red flags that indicate your girl is being bullied at school:

O She pretends to be sick when she is not.

O She loses her appetite and wakes up during the night.

O She is sad without a reason.

O She loses interest in doing well in school.

Any time you notice a marked change in your daughter's behavior, probe into the cause. If she is being bullied, sit down with her and map out some solutions to solve the problem.

Do not call the teachers, the principal, the sheriff's department, the highway patrol, and anyone else you know in law enforcement the first time your daughter comes home and tells you she has been bullied. She will not tell you the next time if you don't stay rational and calmly help her with the problem.

Some good tactics for dealing with a bully include:

- Using the buddy system—that is, working with her friends to try to make a buddy out of the bully. Trading insults or trying to embarrass the bully often escalates the problem.

- Instilling confidence in her via role-playing. At home, have her act out the bully part and you be the strong, confident girl.

- Documenting and recording the bully's behavior with a notebook or a camera phone in case you need to take things to the next level and show proof of the bully's behavior.

The best way to remove the threat of bullies from your girl's life is to tell her about the Greek alphabet. The first letter is alpha, a term researchers use to describe girls who are admired by their peers, as in "alpha girls." The second letter, beta, is used for girls who tag along with the alpha girls as followers or would-be alphas, as in "beta girls." It is the beta girls who most often are the victims of bullies because they appear vulnerable. But there is another type of girl, one who is independent-minded and comfortable with herself. She makes the most of her talents and has big goals in life. That is the gamma girl—an amazing and productive girl who forges ahead, sets an example for others, and enjoys just about every day. And she knows how to solve problems.

Show your daughter how to bring out more of her gamma-girl qualities. Bullies may try to intimidate a gamma girl, but they back off when they realize they are outsmarted, outdone, and outclassed. Have her surround herself with other gamma girls who will support her if an alpha girl directs her meanness in your daughter's direction.

But what if your daughter has bully tendencies herself? That is a problem that needs attention. There are underlying causes for your daughter's bullying tendencies. Take an in-depth look at your family/school situation to find out why your girl might be unhappy or feeling ignored or belittled, and then acting out. Bullies can emerge even in "good" families, especially during adolescence. Remember: If you forbid the bullying but don't uncover what might be leading to it, it is not likely to go away. It will just go underground.

Do not snoop, but listen to how she talks to her classmates and watch how she treats younger girls. If your daughter is younger, in elementary school and perhaps even in to middle school, you can read her texts and check her social media for problematic language and coach her on etiquette and empathy. If your girl is older, invading her privacy by reading her texts can backfire and just make her sneakier about what she posts. Instead, as you drive her and her friends to school, keep your ears tuned. Listen for unkind words about other girls and then take your daughter aside. Tell her it is completely uncool for any girl to add to the tribulations other girls may already be experiencing. Being a mean girl is something that you will not tolerate.

Teach your daughter social media–posting etiquette using the acronym THINK: T= Is it True?; H= Is it Helpful?; I= Is it Inspiring?; N= Is it Necessary?; K= Is it Kind?

CONSTANT CHANGE

As your girl grows up, your role as a parent evolves from meeting her basic needs to teaching her skills to teaching her to let nothing get in her way. During the first few years of her life, that meant making sure she wore a coat and hat in cold weather and sunscreen in the summer. Later, it was teaching her how to protect herself from simpler to more insidious dangers. As your daughter gets older, it may seem that external forces would like to prey on her. But be confident; you can keep them at bay. Meanwhile your girl never stands still. She is constantly in the process of evolving, so there are always more stages and challenges—biological and emotional in nature—for which you want to be prepared.

Important Points to Consider

Parents continue to have a strong influence on their daughter's social development, even as she starts to pull back to be with her friends. As a conscious parent, you will want to keep the following in mind when it comes to your daughter's friendships:

- Try as you might, you cannot handpick your daughter's friends, nor should you. Instead, teach her about good and bad qualities in friends, and teach her how to evaluate how certain friends make her feel about herself.

- Educate yourself on the mean-girl phenomenon in collaboration with your daughter. Teach her warning signs of mean-girl behavior and ways to cope with and combat them.

- Understand that mean-girl behavior is often hidden from the watchful eyes of parents. Instead of snooping through your daughter's every text and post, have periodic "check-in" conversations about social media and online communication to make sure she is posting appropriately and is not a target of cyberbullying.

- Avoid jumping in to rescue your daughter and calling parents or school staff every time your daughter's feelings are hurt. Practice the twenty-four-hour rule: After your daughter reports a social problem, listen and empathize with her concern. Then, wait twenty-four hours and see if she would still like help. Things move quickly in the world of social media and friendships. Often, your daughter will have solved the problem a day later.

○ Understand that bullying is pervasive—not a one-off mean comment but a frequent and consistent pattern of aggression. If your daughter complains of mean-girl behavior from a particular girl over a period of time, you will want to delve deeper into the problem.

 **CHAPTER 8**

Understanding Your Tween

Being a tween—the stage between childhood and the teenage years— can be difficult for a girl. On the one hand, she is trying to separate from her parents' influence and become an independent person. That means letting go of the comfortable and secure hands of her parents or caregivers. On the other hand, she is beginning to experience huge changes in her body, which means she needs her parents more than ever. So expect your daughter's tween years to be turbulent, tumultuous, and with your guidance, terrific. This is an incredibly important time to show your daughter patience, support, and empathy.

Puberty and Menstruation

The time in your girl's life when physical and emotional sexuality develops is called puberty. The word *puberty* has two different Latin origins. One is *pubertas*, meaning "like an adult." The other is *pubescere*, meaning "to grow hair." Puberty usually happens between the ages of ten and fifteen, and refers to the physical changes in your daughter that set the stage for the emotional changes of the next segment in her life, adolescence. Girls experience the start of puberty at different ages, and the entire process can take up to four years.

Most girls begin to show noticeable changes in their bodies, including the growth of breasts, the appearance of pubic and underarm hair, widening of the hips, enlargement of the uterus, and the start of menstruation, between age ten and age twelve. But even some third-graders can exhibit prepuberty signs.

Be sure to tell your daughter about puberty long before it happens, certainly by the time she is eight or nine. Explain that the process of puberty is a miracle, and talk to her about the wonderful physical changes that are ahead. Use side-by-side talk if you are watching TV together and a commercial about sanitary products comes on. Use over-the-shoulder talk if she is in the backseat while you are driving to the store. Just make sure the topic is out in the open and on the table any time she has a question or concern about it. Get her excited about the wonders that will soon take place in her body and clue her in to the specifics.

While the average age of a girl starting her period is twelve and a half, it is normal for some girls to begin menstruating much earlier and others much later. Getting her first period can be traumatic for some girls, so be available with understanding, advice, and some good books on the topic.

PUBERTY PERKS

Becoming more adult-like in her body, looks, and thought is the result of your daughter's puberty. This process is generally thought to be complete when she has regular periods that happen at predictable intervals. Make sure your daughter keeps a record of when the following events happen: spotting, a light menstrual flow, a medium flow, and a heavy flow.

By keeping track of these events she can record the miraculous way her body works, predict her next period, and have lots of supplies on hand. Go to the store and pick up several types of sanitary products—from liners to pads with wings to tampons—give them to her and let her pick through them. In other words, show your daughter that her puberty matters to you and that you will be there to help her and talk about these big changes whenever she needs to.

Encourage your daughter to share what is on her mind about the changes she sees in herself. Tell her everybody handles puberty differently. With your help, she will use this time as a steppingstone and not a stumbling block. Giggle with your girl over any embarrassing experiences during your puberty. Tell her that a few decades ago people did not even discuss the topic of puberty.

About 10 percent of girls experience cramping in their lower abdomen before their periods. That happens because the uterus contracts to release the period flow. Exercise such as walking, jogging, or biking can help. A warm bath or a heating pad can also ease the pain. If the cramps are severe, ask the doctor what medications she recommends.

MENSTRUATION MASTERY

If you are uncomfortable with the topic yourself, load up on pamphlets from the guidance department of your daughter's school. Read them, and then hand them to your girl. To master her menstruation ABCs, she needs to know more than just the clinical definition of menstruation, which is the shedding of the endometrium, or lining, of the uterus. The monthly blood loss varies. About two fluid ounces in total is an approximate norm, with the spacing between periods being, on average, between twenty-four and thirty-five days. But again, there is really no normal period.

Whatever periods your daughter experiences, they are normal for her. In the beginning, she will not be regular, but within a year or two, she will ovulate predictably. Should she, or you, feel something is off kilter, of course, see the doctor.

A NEW DAUGHTER

The many changes your girl experiences, starting in her tweens, will affect all major aspects of her life. This time is an important prelude. She is on the verge of growing up. She can use this time as a starting block for a new emphasis on her academics or a change in her athletic involvement. As her body changes, her thoughts will change, too, from little-girl ones to more mature ones. Her social connections and relationships will also undergo an upheaval. In short, your daughter is on the edge of blossoming into the woman she is meant to be.

This is a wonderful opportunity for you to grow as a parent as well. During puberty, you may find that your daughter's change into a young woman comes with your own feelings of confusion. Some parents begin to feel like their daughter is growing up too fast, and want to hold on to that "little girl" as long as possible. Your daughter's transition from a little girl to a young woman may also bring up feelings from your own experience during puberty as well. Take care to acknowledge your own feelings and keep lines of communication open between you and your daughter as you both adjust to this developmental phase.

Blossoming Sexuality and Crushes

Your daughter's sexuality can be described as her behavior, emotions, and sensations connected with her sex organs. It implies experiencing physical attraction and having control over expressing herself sexually. One problem you may encounter is that these days, sex is mentioned everywhere and often far too casually. So your girl may be more openly curious about her sexuality earlier than girls were in the past.

THE POWER OF SEX

Turn this fact to your advantage. Tell your daughter that while "everyone" now seems to talk casually about sexuality and sex, nothing has changed. Sex still has major emotional, physical, and relationship importance. It is very powerful for good reason—after all, it can create a life!

Maturing sexually is a big part of your daughter's adolescence, so you want to help her prepare. Tell her she may already feel the first stirrings of her emerging sexuality and its amazing power, and that this is her chance to get control of what is happening. Instead of letting herself be pulled blindly by the biological forces within her, she should grab the reins and choose the direction. This is a great time to talk to her about values, emotions, and attitudes.

EMPOWERED GIRL

Explain to your daughter what is happening to her. Like the new leaves and buds a rosebush sprouts in spring, her sexual feelings are an indicator of more growth and beauty on the horizon. Tell her she should revel in her more mature thoughts and feelings, including sexual feelings, if she has them. Many girls will also pay more attention to their appearance and experiment with clothes and makeup at this age.

Although she no longer clamors for hugs and kisses the way she did when she was small, your daughter might still be experiencing "skin hunger." That's what experts call the natural human desire for physical touch that we all experience in different ways throughout our lives. Skin hunger has to be fed just like regular hunger. Be sure to pat your daughter on the shoulder, rub her hand, and stroke the top of her head every so often, so she won't turn to boys prematurely to have them fill that void.

Set aside time to talk only about your daughter's new stage: becoming physically and emotionally mature enough to use the power of her sexuality. Tell her that just as her regular periods started out little by little, so will her sexuality—and with it the associated emotions and feelings. This is the perfect time to discuss the various stages of love with her.

CRUSH COURSE

A crush is an early stage in a girl's development of her ability to eventually love deeply. It can be a sudden, intense liking for someone, have minor proportions, and fade quickly. Or it can be a major experience that sets your daughter's heart racing and gives her a tingly feeling. A crush can happen from afar, as with a movie or music star, or up close, as with the boy next door or the one who sits behind her in class. But no matter what kind it is, rejoice with your daughter over her crush, if she tells you about it. If not, just smile as you observe her "crushing" every time the object of her admiration appears on the TV screen or walks past her at the store. Just as you were happy to see her crawl for the first time as a baby, be glad she is moving in the right direction, and get ready. Boy craziness may be about to start at your house.

FLIRT FACTORS

For many girls your daughter's age, having a crush can segue into flirting. That means, acting in some way on the excitement a crush can bring. By flirting, your girl is letting the other person know she is attracted. Teasing, touching, and otherwise showing an emotional connection with someone are typical signs of flirting. Tell your girl that flirting is done best in small doses, with a glance, a brief touch, or a certain comment. Too much can be misinterpreted by society and her peers as over-the-top. While there is nothing wrong with flirting, everything has a time and place.

While having a crush and being flirtatious are your girl's early attempts to get a grip on her feelings of attraction for another person, she could experience jealousy in the process. Warn her about it. Additionally, tell your daughter to let you know if a boy at her school makes comments about her looks that make her uncomfortable. If he touches her, asks her to look at pornographic pictures, sends her photos of himself naked over the Internet, or sexts her via her cell phone, take action. Sexual harassment is not only wrong, it is also against the law.

What your girl needs from you during her tweens is empowerment. She has control over herself and her life no matter what changes are occurring inside her. The stages of having a crush and flirting, and the emotional highs and lows they bring, are simply two more rungs up the ladder of her growth. With your help she can climb them easily, especially if you equip her with as much information as possible about her emotions.

Hormones and Mood Swings

Puberty starts with the pituitary gland producing hormones to stimulate the ovaries to secrete more estrogen. This process and the resulting physical changes can cause mood swings in your daughter. You can see them for yourself: One day she is her usual self, and the next you feel like a stranger has taken over her body. Suddenly she is sullen and uncommunicative. She acts as if she doesn't know you and seems not to appreciate all you have done for her. Though it may be tough, try to be happy about this development, and grin and bear it. It shows that her body and brain are working as they are supposed to.

Teach coping skills for negative moods, such as exercise, engaging in a favorite activity, listening to music, taking some personal time alone, or talking with a friend or family member about how she is feeling. Avoid pointing out that she is moody, which rarely helps matters. Ask what she needs instead. Talk it out? Space? Distraction with a fun activity? Then honor her choice.

MOODS MATTER

Do allow your girl to blame her moodiness on raging hormones, but do not allow her to take her moods out on you or other people in your home. Be aware that, as a preadolescent, she is doing a most important job every day—growing and separating from you—and expect a pendulum effect in her emotions. At this time, some girls may even get overly emotional, especially if they exhibited the trait of becoming upset by trivial things early on.

But be sure to teach your daughter to get a grip on her emotions and moodiness, and to apologize for any rude behavior resulting from them. Remind her to excuse herself politely from the rest of society when she feels a mood attack coming on. Soon she will be able to predict her cycle of sadness or irritability and be prepared.

PMS STRESS

Some girls feel different before they get their periods, sometimes as early as two weeks before their periods start. They find themselves changing emotionally, crying easily, being grumpy, or wanting to be left alone. They can also have sore breasts, feel puffy, or crave sweets or other foods. This is just another diagnosis for your daughter, if needed, not an alibi. Tell her to look at the calendar and predict when she might experience another episode of premenstrual syndrome, and you might cut her a little slack.

VENTILATION TIME

What can help your girl most is letting her tell you how she feels without rushing her. You might also suggest that she write it all down in her journal or other personal offline log, or that she vent her feelings by chatting or texting with her friends. Tell her to think of emotions as ocean waves. Sometimes all you can do is just stand still and let them wash over you. Allow your daughter some time and space to find her own way back to being the sweet, kind, and caring girl she is. Even the loveliest rose has a thorn or two.

Your girl can also elevate her mood by:

O Reading her favorite book or listening to her music

O Taking a nap with her pet

O Being by herself and doing absolutely nothing for as long as she wants

In short, your daughter needs to acquire her own set of tools for dealing with potential mood swings that can plague some women for decades. Embracing the fact that hormones affect girls differently than boys can make your daughter feel special—and it will, with your support.

Rebellion and Secrets

More and more your tween daughter wants to be her own distinct person and have her own personality, so naturally she pulls away from you. She does this physically, by spending more time with her friends, and psychologically, by rebelling against you. While most parents know that tweens naturally try to pull away from their parents as they get older, the experience of having your girl trying to breaking away from you can be difficult. Instead of thinking of it as a separation, think of your relationship with your tween daughter as an infinity sign. At any given point, you and your daughter may be close together, in the center of the infinity sign, or far apart, on the ends of the infinity sign, but you are always connected.

DEFIANCE

A good way to honor your tween daughter's desire to defy you now and then is to let her have her say in matters that are not important in the long run. Consider her choices of hairstyle, clothing, and fashion. As long as her options are not offensive and against the school dress code, she can go with them.

Be sure your preadolescent daughter has some rules and regulations to rebel against. If there are none in place, she will take her instinct to rebel to school and the community. For a tween, the urge to break rules can be confined to a minimum if it has room to play itself out on the home front.

Do not give in on matters of safety, health, and important values, however. Make it clear to your girl that you will not bend when it comes to her physical, mental, and psychological well-being. But you can do a few important things:

1. **Compromise.** Let your daughter explain to you why she has to stay up until midnight—to attend a concert by a teen idol you approve of, for example. Then have her take a nap before the concert, and another one the day after the concert.

2. **Let her individualize her meals.** She can have dinner food for breakfast and breakfast food for dinner, for example, but she must eat three meals a day.

3. **Let her set her own weekly schedule,** as far as after-school activities are concerned, as long as she schedules some downtime—time for chilling out—on a regular basis.

SECRECY

Keeping secrets is another trait of girls in the tween stage. Suddenly you find your daughter whispering to her best friend and receiving her friend's whispered messages. This is a normal stage among girls that age. Some researchers say it is the precursor of later intimacy, a close, warm relationship with the "absence of fences." In the past, she probably came to you with every little concern. Now you find her discussing all sorts of topics with her friends. Be glad. Do you really care about who had to go to the bathroom twice during social studies? Use a common-sense approach when dealing with your girl's sudden tendency to keep things from you. If your daughter's secrecy worries you, it is time to find out why. You do that best by getting her to open up about it.

Getting Your Daughter to Talk

Talk therapy is very popular, not only on TV but also in the offices of people trained for it. You are also trained for it. Since your girl was little, you have been talking to her regularly, not just about her chores and grades but also about her wishes and hopes. Instead of talking to her less as she gets older, talk to her more. It is therapeutic for both of you.

Up the ongoing talk time with your daughter and don't stop. If she is close-mouthed, find an unthreatening topic to chat about, such as a silly reality TV show. Have fun talking with her about your history. Share the story of when you first liked a girl or boy. Mention your quirky behavior when you were her age.

ONE TIME, MY SISTER . . .

If you cannot talk about yourself, tell your girl about your brother or sister or childhood friends, and how they tried to get a girl or boy interested in them way back when. Exaggerate! The more hilarious the stories are, the better she'll like them. When your girl laughs with you, she momentarily forgets that she has decided not to talk to you anymore. So get her grinning and keep at it. Talk about the end result of the important growth stage she is going through. It will be worth it before long. The successful mastery of one stage of development leads to more success in the future. Chitchat with your girl, or have serious conversations with her. You might also try communicating by phone, through texting, picture-sharing, or e-mailing, or via notes that end with a question, such as "What do you think of . . . ?"

TERRIFIC TWEENS

Without a doubt, you are the most important factor in the equation. Your example, attitude, and determination to make the tween years ten times better for your girl than they were for you are what matter most. You are an involved, conscious parent, so dig into the topic of preadolescence, research how other parents handle this time, and start an e-mail or texting conversation with other moms and dads. Make sure the tween stage is not a time when your daughter slips through the cracks, but rather a time when she gets as much attention as possible.

Jesse Jackson once said, "Your children need your presence more than your presents." He was right. Your girl always needs you more than any gifts you can buy her, no matter how extravagant. But she needs you especially during her preadolescence as she is trying to enter her teenage years that bring with them even more exciting changes, challenges, and conquests.

Important Points to Consider

The tween years are marked by a pendulum-like swing between your daughter retaining her "little girl" qualities and showing increasingly more mature behavior. It is an exciting time for your daughter, and you can enjoy it with her by keeping the following in mind:

○ This time period is full of physical changes that you will want to prepare her for. She may begin puberty and start her period. Conversations about what is happening and what will happen to her body will ease the transition.

○ Recognize that hormonal changes may affect your daughter's mood and behavior to some extent. Instead of mourning the time when she was younger and free of mood swings, learn to be present with her and help her develop coping skills to ride them out.

○ If your daughter is moody, ask her what she needs, or give her a "menu" of options that can get her out of her funk. She may just need time by herself, rest, exercise, distraction, or an opportunity to talk things out with you or her friends. Respect her choices in how she learns to cope.

○ Keep lines of communication open. While she is looking more mature these days, she still has immature problem-solving skills. Be a resource for her and let her know you may not be able to solve her problems, but you are open to being an empathetic listener and thought partner with her.

○ Be aware that your communication may extend beyond face-to-face interaction into the world of texting and digital communication.

CHAPTER 9

The World of the Teenage Girl

Your daughter's teen years are the last she'll spend before being welcomed into adulthood. You've spent a great deal of time supporting your daughter and helping her become a strong young woman; don't allow anything to damage or undo the good work you've done with her so far. Being especially conscious in your parenting is crucial during this development period. Take advantage of the fact that your daughter is now an almost fully realized adult by discussing her future with her, and staying engaged and present as often as possible.

Teaching Her Media Smarts

As a teenager, your daughter has important work to do, in addition to going to school and doing everything else she does. Being an adolescent is a learning process that revolves around becoming an adult. Your daughter will pass through this period with flying colors if—at the end of her teens—she can joyfully answer the question, "Who am I?" to her satisfaction and to yours.

However, before your daughter can do that with any certainty, she—like all girls her age—may go through a few years of floundering. During this time she may engage in the following activities:

○ Experiment with various pretend personas, even negative or delinquent ones.

○ Try out these personas to see if any of them are a good fit for her.

○ Find one that is most suited to her and revel in it.

During this key trial-and-error process your teenage daughter truly needs you more than ever. She wants and seeks your leadership and guidance to become a successful teen.

THE "MESS" MEDIA

The mass media—consisting of newspapers, magazines, TV, radio, movies, and blogs—have become very powerful during the past few decades. In fact, these days, television, advertising, and the latest technology permeate every corner of life. For example, most homes have more than one TV, as well as computers, video games, webcams, digital recording devices, and the latest requisite accoutrements. Thus, the mass media influence every facet of today's existence. To add to matters, current trends and popular opinion can spread like wildfire through social media, and the lines between advertising, fact, and opinion are blurred at best.

Whether you like it or not, your daughter will become ensnared in whatever fabric the mass media weave when they portray teens. In regard to girls, that fabric is often messy or just plain flawed. The media often portray girls as rebellious, disrespectful, self-centered, and superficial. Worse, they show girls as precocious or "slutty."

Girls want to be pointed in the right direction, but the mass media are not the place for that. Powered by a profit-making mentality, they zoom in on your girl as a fresh new consumer with deep pockets and plenty of desires to fit in. With the right education, you can teach your daughter to be a critical consumer.

MASS MEDIA MASTERY

You do not take your responsibility as a parent lightly. You know that forewarned is forearmed, and forearmed is unharmed. Therefore, you want your daughter to be prepared for the onslaught of deceptive advertising that she experiences each day via the mass media. In our culture, there is not only an ever-growing expectation and belief that teenage girls are flighty, but there are also marketing gurus at work who decree that it is to our economy's advantage that adolescent girls be more concerned with their appearance, their relationships with others, and approval from men than with their own ideas, expectations, and achievements.

With every teen magazine or blog that girls read, they are bombarded with the message that their minds are less important. It is their looks, their bodies, and their emerging "sex appeal" that matter most. In short, the mass media are valuing teenage girls less as people and more as purchasers. Use this fact as a great tool for informing your daughter. Tell her that as far as she is concerned, it is a buyer's market. She is a hot commodity. The advertisers—whether on TV, on the radio, in print, or on the Internet—are desperately trying to market their products, services, and a certain lifestyle to her. While the commercials and ads can be considered a form of free expression, the methods they are using are often misleading. With your help, however, your daughter can examine closely the types of ads and commercials aimed at her, the overt messages behind them, and the hidden implications.

You will both laugh as you channel surf and check out some commercials. Flip through the ad sections of your newspaper and scan the glossy portions meant for girls. "Buy me, buy me, buy me," all the advertisements scream. On every website, there is a chance to buy something that will supposedly make her more popular and attractive. Soon your daughter will discover that there is a big imbalance, with her, an informed teenager, holding all the power. She is the one who can pick and choose. The marketers can only lose.

In her book *Cinderella Ate My Daughter*, Peggy Orenstein writes about how to equip your daughter to combat the outrageous expectations the media place on how she should look: stress what your daughter's body can do over how it looks; praise her for accomplishments; involve her in team sports; encourage volunteerism, which can give her perspective and purpose; and teach media literacy to raise her awareness about marketers' manipulations.

Internet Safety Basics for Teens

The most important computer basic is the skill to use it successfully and with respect. While tests show that kids who have TVs in their bedrooms score lower on exams, those who have access to computers score higher. So without a doubt, the Internet can open a door to a vast arena of information and entertainment for your teenage girl, but only with your involvement. Without close supervision, the Internet can do much more harm than good.

Therefore, welcome all the positives the Internet offers, but be alert to its potential for enormous negatives. Most parents do not realize that the Internet can be considered a gate to and from your home, with the door always wide open. No matter how many safety features and parental controls you install and upgrade regularly, someone somewhere will be able to get around any firewalls or other protective measures you add to your computer, come right in, and visit your daughter—and that someone often has predatory intentions. So do not set up the computer in your girl's bedroom. Set it up in the den or kitchen, where you can keep a watchful eye.

Too many criminals consider the Internet their personal trawling grounds for prey. These days, new Internet criminals pop up every day. Make sure your daughter is not gullible, and don't be lulled into a false sense of security because she is school-smart. Too many girls can be too trusting when it comes to online connections and end up in harm's way.

Tell your daughter never to hand out any personal information, phone numbers, addresses, credit card numbers, or the name or details of her school to anyone online. Quite a few sites enable a user to find a street address by entering a phone number, or a school by entering the size of its student population and state.

COMPUTER RULES

Instruct your daughter on how to avoid all Internet dangers. She should never open an e-mail or attachment from someone she does not know. Talk to her about the dangers of phishing sites (sites pretending to be other sites that look exactly the same). Discuss and post computer rules with your daughter, or she will assume that there are no rules. Some rules you will want to discuss with her include:

- ☐ Location of technology use
- ☐ Screen times and technology curfews
- ☐ Grounds for checking her technology
- ☐ Conditions for removal of technological privileges

Each family will be different in their technology policies, but it is important for the family to decide and agree upon the rules. You should also lead by example. If you have a rule, "No technology at the dinner table" and you check a text during a meal, your teenager will notice the hypocrisy right away.

Chances are, as she gets older, she will be incredibly tech-savvy and be able to clear her search history and keep her online world private from you. She may even resent you for "invading" her privacy. However, tell her it is your job to keep her safe, both online and offline.

COMPUTER CONSEQUENCES

If your daughter breaks your computer rules, ask for an explanation. She may have clicked on something accidentally. If she continues to visit dangerous sites, however, you will have to do what you would if—when the times comes—she drives unsafely. You would take away her driving privileges then. So, restrict her computer use to only homework, with you looking over her shoulder. In all likelihood, it will not come to that.

Discuss the rise of three new Internet crimes with your daughter: cyber stalking—stalking a person over the Internet by tracking her every move; cyber impersonation—assuming a different gender, age, and appearance, such as an older male pretending to be a lonely young girl wanting to be friends; and identity theft, which can occur when a stranger steals her Social Security number and runs up huge debts in her name.

LIFETIME CYBER RISKS

It is not only the threat of questionable characters gaining access to your daughter via the Internet that you want to warn her about. Her decision to share something about herself with the cyber universe can also have bad consequences. Naïve kids can indeed risk their futures as potential college students, scholarship recipients, or employees if they are careless in what they post online.

There are several ad-supported services that are very popular with young people. Most likely, your daughter and her friends already use social networking sites and apps such as Facebook, Snapchat, Instagram, and Twitter. If so, warn her about the illusion of privacy. Whatever she posts about herself may come back to haunt her. These days, companies planning to hire her, even just for a summer job or an internship, may enter her name not only into a search engine but also on the various social networks.

Keep in mind that sometimes the greatest online threat to your daughter is not a stranger lurking in the shadows of the Internet but her own classmates and friends. Having someone post mean comments about her can feel devastating to her. Teach her to come to you if she is being harassed online by peers.

Lauri Sybel, a career development professional, advises students to think of their social-networking pages as a job application or résumé. She has seen many instances of students being rejected from internships or jobs because of pictures posted of them "partying" on a social-networking page.

Music Mania and Hollywood

Two more areas to be wary of, in regard to your teen girl and her healthy development, are popular music and Hollywood. Both can present false images. While you cannot understand why your girl loves a certain song, you must keep in mind that this situation is centuries old. Think of the type of music you adored when you were an adolescent and how it shocked your elders. They shook their heads in disgust at what they called "that awful noise," as in, "Turn off that awful noise—now!" As a teenager, you thought your parents did not understand "good music." Now it is your turn to be baffled by your daughter's selections on the radio or what she downloads.

Do not—like a broken record—repeat your parents' mantra about the "awful noise." Doing so will only alienate you from her world. Listen to your girl's music first. Maybe you can get an inkling of what makes it so popular in her opinion. Perhaps it is the beat or the background sounds, but pay attention to the lyrics, too. If you are not a fan of the latest music trends, get ready to be shocked.

NIX NAME-CALLING

Do you allow your daughter to be called ugly names? Of course not. So express to your daughter that you have concerns about verbal degradation of women or the description of violence toward them, no matter how enticing the melody or rhythm. However, clamping down and restricting her music may have the opposite effect of making it more alluring to her, and making you seem like you are out of touch. While you cannot avoid all songs that have negative messages, you can talk with your daughter about why the messages are offensive. You might also seek out the "clean" radio versions of songs that are better alternatives.

HOLLYWOOD

Often, the movie industry uses women only as décor, and makes a huge profit from hyper-sexualizing young girls. Of course, like any commercial venture, Hollywood is profit-based. Ask your girl to read the movie reviews carefully before heading to the theater. Allow her to flex her discerning mind muscles as to what films she'd like to see.

Watch some chick flicks with your daughter and enjoy discussing what in the movie was factual or based on reality. In those discussions, it will become obvious that, slowly but surely, your girl is getting better at judging what is real and what is just "reel."

Real Life versus Reel Life

Watch any movie or a fashion show on TV, and you can see at a glance that these days incredibly thin actresses and emaciated models dominate the screen. Most of them thinner than is healthy for them. What you should worry about is the negative impact all that skinniness has on your daughter.

Girl's dissatisfaction with their bodies starts at an alarmingly young age. Recent studies found that over 80 percent of 10-year-old girls are afraid of being fat. By middle school, 40–70 percent of girls are dissatisfied with two or more parts of their body, and body satisfaction is at an all-time low between ages 12 and 15, which coincides with puberty. At the same time, your daughter is being bombarded by unrealistic standards of beauty and thinness in the media, which can fuel their dissatisfaction. Make sure your daughter is able to separate what she sees via a movie reel from what is real. She is a real girl with many fascinating activities on her plate, many great concepts to learn, and a fabulous future ahead. While appearance does not have to be the last item on her list, it should definitely not be her first and only one.

Encouraging Healthy Relationships

Worshiping underweight actresses and starving models is unhealthy. Make sure your girl's life is filled with people she can adore who present a healthy image for her. Introduce her to young businesswomen, artists, athletes, and coaches. Teach her to be proud of the way she looks, be it in sneakers or heels. Tell her—over and over—that she is the daughter you always wanted and how proud of her you are.

What is of utmost importance for your girl is to develop a healthy relationship with reality and with herself. She needs to understand both the pull of independence and her need to remain grounded in her parents' domain.

UNDERSTANDING INDEPENDENCE

To assert her ever-increasing independence, your daughter must put a measure of distance between herself and you. That is a good development. Welcome it. On days when your daughter is easy to guide and she listens to every word you have to offer with appreciation, you feel gratified. On other days, when she seems to develop strange tastes and goes for idol worshiping that is foreign to you, you may feel that whatever you tell her falls on deaf ears. Never retreat and pout when your daughter impatiently tells you, "I know, I know. You've told me about this a million times." Just smile and say, "It's my job!" Instill in your daughter the unwavering certainty that amid whatever changes she goes through emotionally and physically as a teenager, you are her permanent post of encouragement and safety. You are her handrail and her first and best support system—always available and never closed.

Handling the Teenage Years with Grace

Parents today have a unique set of challenges when it comes to parenting teens. Technology and social media can dominant a teen's worlds. Even the most technological savvy parent can have trouble keeping up with their teenage daughter's life online. Balancing between being involved in her online choices while not violating privacy can be difficult. Parents may also feel disconnected from their daughter as she branches into an online world and technology independence without them. It is important to remember that when you were a teenager, you did not share everything with your parents, and nor should your daughter. If she is developing appropriately, she will be gravitating toward her friends (online and in real life). The most important thing is for parents to keep the lines of communication open and in moments of disconnection, remember the infinity sign—always connected, but to different degrees. Pulling away is normal, and you can seek comfort in the fact that she knows that you are there for her when she comes back.

Important Points to Consider

Psychologist and educator G. Stanley Hall once described adolescence as a period of "storm and stress," but having a teenage daughter does not have to be that way. It is, however, a time in which you must continue to be aware of the risks that are unique to teenagers and teach your daughter how to navigate them. With your support, she will get through her teenage years and emerge as a young adult with confidence and resilience to solve whatever challenge comes her way. As you walk this journey with her, keep in mind the following:

O Teaching your daughter media smarts and media literacy is of utmost importance. You may not be able to restrict what she watches, reads online or in print, or sees in advertising, but you can educate her on media manipulation and being a critical consumer.

O Know that media messages, when left unchecked, can contribute to teenage girls holding unnatural expectations for how their bodies should look, which can be damaging to their self-image.

O Protecting your daughter from dangers on the Internet starts with setting ground rules together. Talk about the important technology rules your family will follow and set a good example in following them yourself.

O Be aware that the Internet is a powerful and wonderful tool, but without guidance, your daughter may fall prey to its dangers. In addition to strangers trying to steal your daughter's financial and personal information, there is also the risk of her leaving a permanent digital footprint during a lapse of judgment, such as if she posts something inappropriate or hurtful about someone, or others post hurtful things about her. Teach her digital etiquette and safety precautions.

O Keep the lines of communication open about technology by keeping up with the latest apps, websites, and social media to the best of your ability. You cannot protect her from what you don't know.

 **CHAPTER 10**

Father-Daughter Relationships

The relationship between a girl and her father is special and deserves to be treated as such. It is most often the first male-female relationship in a girl's life and can form the foundation for how your daughter approaches her future relationships with men. Many men feel awkward dealing with a growing daughter, but your interactions with her are pivotal in her life. From this relationship, your daughter develops a sense of self-acceptance. Since a child tends to regard herself as others regard her, her father's view is very important. But the father-daughter bond has many more beneficial aspects. If it is strong and healthy, it sends your daughter into the world with clear and healthy expectations for men. Spend time helping build your daughter's confidence in herself and her capabilities, and she'll continue those techniques throughout her life.

One-on-One Time with Dad

One benefit a daughter gets from relating to her father is a healthy concept of self. Your daughter learns to feel good about herself in part through her interactions with you, her father. She reasons that if you respect her as she is, she must be worthy of that respect and acts accordingly.

Your role as father grows and changes over time, but starting early will set a stronger foundation for deepening your relationship in the future. Therefore, your daughter needs to get as much meaningful time with you as she can beginning early on. Make it a definite and specific part of her everyday experiences. "Dad time" does not always just happen. It must be scheduled, just like other important things. How do you accomplish this?

O Set aside a special few minutes every day for your daughter to spend with you and you alone. Call it out as "dad-daughter" time, and make a point to put aside all distractions, including your phone, e-mails, and thoughts about other things, and just be fully present with her. Allow her to pick what you do during this time.

O Once a month, go on a special outing with just you and your daughter. It can be as simple as going on a bike ride together, going out to eat, or taking in a movie together.

O Make sure your daughter has a chance every day to eat at least one meal with you.

O Be sure to take part in your daughter's bedtime ritual.

O Encourage your daughter to come to you for advice.

If for some reason you can't do dad-daughter time one day, be honest with your daughter and make sure to reschedule the time with her. Sometimes life happens, and teaching your daughter to be flexible while still holding you to a certain standard will help her grow as an individual.

MORE THAN ONE FATHER

If you are not your daughter's biological father, honor her connection to him. As her "second" or "real" father—in the sense that you are raising her—you should not overlook the original bond between your girl and her birth father. In this situation, it is even more important to plan ahead for those occasions when your daughter and her biological dad can spend time together. While that time may be limited, there are other ways to make the connection between her and her original father strong. The same goes for you if you are divorced and your daughter lives with a stepfather, maybe even far away. Insist on seeing her as much as possible.

Whether your daughter is being raised primarily by another man, whether you are the girl's stepfather and part of her everyday life, or whether you are raising your biological daughter, remember the importance of the father-daughter bond and do all you can to make it strong and vibrant. The best tactics go beyond any "hurt-feelings" game playing between adults and focus solely on what's best for the girl. Some examples of helpful strategies include the following:

- Inform the biological father regularly of your custodial daughter's progress and insisting the same is done for you, should you be the noncustodial dad.

- Have her develop a strong phone, e-mail, and texting relationship with you and with her biological dad. Encourage her to use Skype or Facetime (video-phone services) with her biological dad, if possible.

- Plan a frequent weekend ritual with your daughter that will not be deviated from unless absolutely necessary.

- Set up vacation and holiday plans that include specific times for your daughter to spend more time with you, whether you are her biological dad or her custodial dad.

If both a biological father and a stepfather are in the picture, the scheduling can be tricky, but don't worry. You, as the girl's father—no matter how you came to assume this role—can put yourself in your daughter's shoes and remember what is best for her. So split up the vacations and holidays, or alternate the destinations. Be flexible and have your girl spend some time with you and some time with her other father.

Reconfigured Father Figure

Only through a father figure can a daughter learn what it means to be female in relationship to a male. But don't feel defeated if you cannot be present in your daughter's life on a daily basis. Modern life has made our existence much more complex. You want to be a strong father to your daughter and spend much time with her, but if that's not possible, just remember: Your girl's father time can be a composite, made up of several regular periods spent with several different men who all have something positive to contribute to her. If you can't attend all her volleyball games, swim meets, and play rehearsals, maybe her uncle or your male cousin can step up. Be resourceful in including a good male role model in her life.

Many men were brought up in an environment that suppressed their flow of emotions. That does not mean they don't feel; it means only that they are afraid to reveal their inner selves. By making sure you are a part of as many events and stages of your daughter's life as possible, you can get closer to her. Also, you will know in the future that you did all you could.

Just as your girl benefits from time with you, so do you benefit from time with her. Little girls help their fathers see the world through the eyes of a girl. If you are truly present in your little girl's life, she will tell you exactly what occupies her mind, thereby widening your horizons. You, in turn, will be enriched by her presence. Your conversations with her will become very special to her. Whatever you tell her will have a deep meaning in her life.

By choosing what messages to send to your daughter, you can greatly influence her self-esteem. She looks to you as her first and most important source of validation.

Self-Esteem Building via Dad

It is crucial that you help build your daughter's self-esteem. Low self-esteem can undermine your daughter's desire to achieve, can affect her negatively throughout life, and may lead to depression. Even if she turns out to become a high achiever, her self-esteem in other areas is also extremely important. Self-esteem is not an all-or-nothing phenomenon—one can feel accomplished and proud in different areas—friendships, being a part of a community, athletics, arts, and so forth.

> Keep your positive attention on your daughter's accomplishments and personality over how she looks. As the first significant man in her life, it is crucial that you take an interest in the many facets of your daughter. A compliment about her looks here and there is not forbidden, of course, but it should be balanced with other key messages about her inner beauty.

Fortunately, these days the number of fathers trying to do their best by their daughters is increasing, even though they may have trouble with the issues of personal relationships.

A FATHER'S CHALLENGE

In the book *Raising Cain: Protecting the Emotional Life of Boys*, psychologists Dan Kindlon and Michael Thompson refer to the challenging gender gap between mothers and sons that can translate later into a man's problematic emotional existence.

Fathers of girls, however, face an even more challenging gender gap when trying to connect with their daughters, according to educator and psychologist JoAnn Deak. In her book *Girls Will Be Girls: Raising Confident and Courageous Daughters*, she points out that mothers, being women, are generally better equipped with relationship skills and, in that way, better prepared for their parenting jobs. In contrast, men as fathers do not have the best emotional equipment for their task of raising a girl and may have to struggle with it. But what a great payoff they reap by making an effort.

A FATHER'S CHOICE

By making a deliberate effort, you can overcome your own parents' child-rearing shortcomings and build a loving and lasting relationship with your daughter. The decision to commit to making a connection with your daughter is all you need to get started. Your presence and uniqueness will guide you in the right direction. All you have to do is be yourself and be willing to share a part of yourself.

You should never tell your daughter that she is eating too much or getting fat, even if you are just trying to be helpful. Instead, you can focus on helping her make healthy choices, such as eating a well-balanced diet and being active for her health (rather than for her looks alone).

Your strengths can show themselves in many ways:

- If you are inclined to be funny, be goofy with your daughter, play silly games with her, and make her laugh.

- If you like to tell stories, start telling her a tale of adventure—or read one to her—that has many installments, which you can narrate to her daily over the course of weeks or months.

- If you are the quiet type, ask your daughter to tell you the names of all her stuffed toys and fill you in on the background of each one.

- If you like to sing, ask her to teach you the songs she learns at school and sing along with her.

○ With an older daughter, you can take on a project together, whether it is something around the house or a project she is involved in at school or in her clubs.

Whatever your personality, you can use it to strengthen your bond with your daughter. She will appreciate all your attempts, especially if you establish a pattern in your interactions with her and are reliable and trustworthy. This will teach her to be reliable and trustworthy, too.

Even if you are a very busy man, make time for your daughter. If you have little free time, you can include your girl whenever you do your chores at home. Even when your daughter becomes a preteen and teen, she needs to spend time with you on a regular basis. You should never take "Leave me alone!" as a signal that your daughter no longer needs you. You should take it for what it is—a temporary breather in your girl's dependence on you.

The more time you devote to spending with your girl, the more her confidence rises. The most important man in her life enjoys her company. That makes her feel important not only in your eyes—and the world's—but also in her own. Yet besides raising your daughter's self-esteem, you play another crucial role in your daughter's development.

Role Modeling: Your Daughter's Boyfriends

You are the role model for the types of boys your daughter may become attracted to. Through your behavior and actions, she will learn two important things that may affect her happiness for the rest of her life:

1. Which male characteristics to rate highly, treasure, and try to find in a potential boyfriend

2. Which male characteristics to rate poorly, reject, and be sure to avoid in a potential boyfriend

Besides getting firsthand knowledge about a man's good and not-so-good qualities, your girl will also get her first introductory lesson in the possibilities of romantic love between a man and a woman by watching how you treat her mother and other women in your life.

Therefore, you should exhibit your best side not only in front of your daughter but also in front of your mate. When you treat your daughter's mother like a queen, your daughter feels like a princess. When you compliment her mother, you compliment your daughter. When you praise her mother, you extol your daughter.

The same goes for how you treat your own mother. If you make it a point to be loving around her and your wife, your daughter learns that a man is supposed to be loving, how he shows that love appropriately, and what she needs to expect from a future mate.

> You and your mate should spend as much time in your roles of husband and wife, or as a couple, as possible. Making your relationship as solid and as permanent as you can helps your daughter realize that a good and lasting relationship is possible. This will become a top goal for her future.

Whenever possible, you should show your love to the mother of your girl by expressing your fond feelings through whatever means you think best (flowers, cards, etc.). Flowing from that might be a special surprise for your daughter (such as tucking her favorite snack into her lunchbox), your compliments to her about her abilities (such as remarking about her keeping her room neat), and your recognition of her talents (such as displaying her artwork in your office).

ROLE-MODELING MOTHER

Your girl's mother should do her part as well in building a good father-daughter relationship by praising your outstanding qualities, by showing your daughter a photo of herself and you when you two met, and by telling your girl what makes you special and what attracted her to you in the first place. Thus, the father-daughter relationship—realized to the extent of its rich potential—can offer great benefits to every member of the family.

In families where there are both girls and boys, make sure you do not invest more time and energy in the relationships with your sons than in the relationships with your daughters. If daughters are relegated to a second-class status, they will never forget it, and the sons will grow up to perpetuate the unfairness.

Through your daily actions and attempts to understand your daughter you will show her that you love her unconditionally. Plus, you will instruct her in how a fine man acts. Your example of masculinity is something she will use as a measuring stick in her future relationships with other males. If she has been taught well, she will do her best to find a good mate. You can help her in this by encouraging her early boyfriends to come to the house. As she gets older, you can teach her that she should expect respect from boys, the same kind of respect you always show her mother. You also must make certain that she will know when she is *not* being treated well.

Sharing Your Daughter's Passions

Society tends to define young girls by their activities, such as: She is an equestrian, a softball player, or a gymnast. You should make sure your daughter has something positive in her life by which her friends and community can define her. Ask her what her passion is and help her explore it more deeply. Often that passion revolves around a sport she is drawn to. You can use this activity to teach her more self-control and patience.

You model self-discipline by the way you act, and you foster your daughter's self-discipline and control by her involvement in something that demands:

- Practicing a skill for a long time, such as playing golf or tennis

- Working on a long-range project, such as building a piece of furniture

- Investing much of her time and money in something, such as starting a collection

You can also observe any natural athletic talent your daughter may have and build on the passion she feels for the sport. You can coach your girl or, by following your own passion, guide her into rooting for your favorite teams, or get her to imitate your own sports prowess if she shows an interest. She may end up loving something you excelled in or take the sport to a whole new level.

Remember that you should always include both your boys and girls in the sports training you provide and the sports equipment you install in your backyard. In fact, you should make no distinction between how much time you devote to your son's little league games and your daughter's track meets. You never want your daughter to feel less worthy as an athlete because of scheduling. Also don't limit your daughter's presents to traditional "girl" items. You can offer your daughter more "masculine" gifts, such as a baseball mitt or a chemistry set, and see if she enjoys them. It's not about pushing one type of gendered activity upon her; it's about giving her a wide array of interests from which she can choose.

You can teach your daughter many valuable life lessons through sports, such as how not to take tryouts too seriously, how to be a good winner and a good loser, and how to throw herself into a pursuit she loves just for the sake of it. Hobbies can also create a close connection between fathers and daughters.

SHARING HOBBIES

Above all, share an interest that allows you and your daughter to keep up with each other over time. There is always an occasion to talk during a fishing trip—at least during the drive to the lake and back home—or a camping excursion. Traveling together, by bike, by boat, by car, on foot, or even with her on your shoulders or in a carrier when she is little can also nurture your father-daughter connection. During those travels, you and your girl will have many chances to solve problems. You can teach your daughter how to create something out of nothing, or how to make the best out of any situation, no matter how bad. One example is calling a flat tire an opportunity for adventure. Documenting your travels and putting them on a flash drive, rehashing your trips and creating a blog, or videotaping your visits to the zoo or the planetarium will give her many precious memories.

SHARING HOPES

Spending an evening with you gazing at the stars will nurture your girl's sense of awe. As you explain your view of the universe, and your hopes and dreams for her, she will feel free to tell you of her hopes and dreams while developing a commitment to being the best she can be. Things worth doing and realizing one's dreams can take a lot of time and work, but each step along the way, you can help your daughter soar. This may also be a good time to reflect on the positive ways you have grown as a parent. Don't forget to acknowledge your own hard work once in a while.

Inspiring Her to Aim High

You play a pivotal role in your daughter's academic achievement and ambitions. If you introduce her to brain teasers and strategic games like chess early on, have her solve mazes and riddles, she will learn to use her head and be proud. Together, you and your daughter can do crossword puzzles or Sudoku. Reading with her and talking about what she is reading are also great opportunities for bonding and learning.

The more your daughter has a chance to think, the more her capacity for thought will grow. This capacity underlies all learning and has a long shelf life. In fact, clear thinking is the foundation on which all schoolwork builds. Your actions now can be a great impetus in furthering this ability.

FOSTERING HER ASPIRATIONS

There are several ways you can inspire your daughter to grow mentally and reach for her potential. Remember the adage, "You can't be what you can't see." You are an important "tour guide" of her future opportunities. You can explore several possible career paths with her, long before she enters high school, by taking her to visit places where those careers are practiced. You can show her how to research some topics of interest on the Internet. You can send her postcards and e-mails from your business trips, text her snapshots, bring back maps from where you were, and take her to work to show her how you spend your time away from home.

ENCOURAGE HER CURIOSITY

Most importantly, encourage your daughter's curiosity and avoid squelching it. When she asks you something, tell her where to find the answer, if you do not know it. You should also take your daughter to hear inspiring lecturers—male or female, young or old—who can thrill girls with motivational pep talks that make them eager to acquire more knowledge. Be sure to let her overhear you in discussions with other people and ask for her opinions.

Take your daughter on a stroll across the campus of the nearest university, walk with her to the philosophy department, and show her where college students spend their time inquiring into the nature of things. Tell her that many powerful ideas are still waiting to be conceptualized and that you hope that she will not only have such ideas but also be willing to express them to others. Introduce her to some famous women in history, so that she will feel the power of the strong women who have gone before her move through her.

If your connection to your daughter is strong, you can expect her to flourish. Your inspiration will produce great results. She will stand on tiptoes mentally, constantly reaching for new ideas or new understanding. The more often she does that, the more she will enjoy the process. Trust that you can stimulate your daughter's thoughts and visions of her future success more than anyone else in the world. To realize as much of that success as possible, she needs to be determined, have an independent mind, and be strong willed.

Making Girls Strong Willed

Besides helping your daughter think for herself, you should make sure she has a strong will. By giving her many avenues to express herself in word and action, and by not stifling her, you can increase her determination. Teaching your girl that obstacles are only opportunities for increasing her resourcefulness is important. Overall, the most crucial thing for you to remember is that the lessons you teach her when she is little need to last and help her long after you are gone. So your goal is to make your daughter so strong and powerful that she can apply your lessons as the years pass and tackle the problems of the whole world someday, if she chooses to.

For that she needs to learn to use the phrase "I think" often and openly express what she believes. She also needs to be strong enough to put her ideas into action.

O She needs to accept the responsibility of the task at hand and see it through.

O She needs to be able to assert her beliefs and disagree with others, even her superiors in the future, without being unpleasant or becoming aggressive.

O She needs to be able to realize that because she is smart and strong willed, she has an opportunity to put her talents to the best possible use and give back to the community when she is an adult.

Important Points to Consider

As a father, you have a tremendous influence on your daughter. You inspire her to aim higher and to choose the course of her life. In return, she will give you her best efforts and something even more precious. With your conscious involvement, she will grow into an independent, self-confident adult who can easily relate to males and will gravitate toward men who respect her and treat her as an equal. Keep in mind the following points about fatherhood:

○ Don't feel too much pressure to be the world's most perfect father. Just having you in her daily life will make your daughter stronger as a young woman and better able to handle life.

○ Set aside time every day to spend with your daughter one-on-one. Put aside all distractions and just be fully present with her.

○ Be a good role model for your daughter by treating the women in your life with respect. By doing so, you are imprinting on her how she should expect to be treated by men in her life in the future.

○ Involve your daughter in your hobbies and interests and foster and support hers. You don't have to love the same things to connect with each other. Your full attention and presence in her life and her activities will be special to her.

**CHAPTER 11**

Mother-Daughter Relationships

The mother-daughter relationship can be one of the most amazing and magical relationships in the world. It can be exponentially better than any other relationship, because it interconnects two people who have a similar talent—the ability to share their emotions and feelings—and yet are a generation apart. Therefore, one of them has the wisdom of experience and years, and the other has the freshness of youth and yearning. Remember the lifetime of knowledge you have to share with your daughter, and relish the time you spend making new memories with her and learning new things about yourself. With a healthy bond, a mother and her daughter may find that they have the skills and smarts to overcome any problem or challenge they face.

Clashes and Challenges

The special relationship between a mother and daughter is primal, as it is the first one the daughter experiences. As she matures, the daughter starts focusing more on her friends and later perhaps on an emotional partner, but her original love connection is always with her mother. After all, she receives so much from her mom—food, shelter, and nurturing, to name just a few things. From babyhood on, a girl also consciously or subconsciously patterns herself after her mother in speech, mannerisms, and other means of expression. Of course that can cause clashes and challenges.

One of the most common problems between mothers and daughters is the fight over control. The daughter feels that the mother is always trying to control her, and the mother has trouble accepting her little girl as an independent adult. Also many mothers are not sure of who they are and how they feel about themselves as people, so they focus all their energies on the person their daughter is turning out to be. A mother who is secure and comfortable as a person will be a better role model for a daughter than a mother who is constantly badgering a daughter to improve herself.

Two headstrong women who are only one generation apart can have many disagreements and end up in a battle based on control and rebellion. Remember: What worked for you will not always work for your daughter, but you must set a pattern early on of problem-solving and settling any disagreements with her. This pattern should include compromising, laying out the pros and cons of a decision she has to make, and admitting it when you were wrong.

RESOLVE CLASHES

The more often the process of conflict resolution between you and your daughter occurs, the smoother the relationship will be. But even then difficulties can arise. One major stumbling block is the silent treatment. Ditch it at all costs. Silence does nothing but erect a wall, or create an abyss, between you and your girl. As a conscious parent, communication is the best tool you have in your arsenal. Keep communicating even if your daughter turns mum. If you find yourself hesitating to open your mouth for fear of saying something to her you will regret later, turn to a notepad, your computer, or a text message first. By writing down what is on your mind, you have a chance to examine the words before you show or send them to your daughter. When you speak, the thought process is often minimal, because words can fly out of your mouth. But the simple act of committing your thoughts to a sheet of paper, a computer, or a cell phone slows down the communication process and helps to ensure that your message will be clear and productive.

Keeping Communication Open

If your daughter isn't thrilled about finding herself saddled with some of your quirks, do not take it personally. If she does not accept everything she inherited from your side, it shows she is at least thinking and talking about her existence versus yours. In fact, it is good for your girl to reject things in you that you have not yet resolved. However, if you look at life as a wonderful smorgasbord of opportunities and communicate these feelings, your daughter is more likely to feel that way, too.

It is your job to initiate the flow of communication after your daughter has cut it off. If you do not make the effort, both of you will feel helpless and hopeless. You are the adult. Give your daughter power by showing her that you are not afraid to tackle a touchy subject or whatever stands between you. It is always a sign of strength to broach a difficult topic. But verbalizing hurt feelings can be tricky.

The way you talk to your daughter becomes her inner voice. No mother is perfect and able to convey all positive messages all the time, but you want to be aware that labeling your child with your words (e.g., lazy, stubborn, disrespectful) can have an impact on her beliefs about herself. The words you choose matter. Every child (and person!) has moments of feeling lazy (versus *being* a lazy person). Stubbornness is determination and persistence in disguise. Disrespect is an opportunity to teach her different ways to disagree and assert herself.

Remember when communicating with your daughter that your tone of voice and facial demeanor can carry just as much weight as the words you choose. You never want to come across as overly critical. In some cases, writing rather than speaking your feelings is the best choice; the written word, thought out beforehand, is much more neutral. The sharpest thorns in the hearts of grown women are the unkind words their own mothers said to them. Make sure you do not pierce your daughter's core with careless or unkind remarks. If unkind words come out in the heat of the moment, when the dust has settled, take ownership and apologize to her. This will teach her to do the same when she accidentally lashes out.

LIGHT TOUCHES

Whenever you two have different opinions, take a deep breath and rehearse something nice to say before launching into what upsets you about your daughter. If you cannot find the right words, you can always:

O Dash off an e-mail to your daughter, send her a joke, or text her a greeting.

O Chat online with her about a book that has nothing to do with your current conflict and everything to do with your determination to keep communication open.

Texting offers three functions that are of great use in parenting. First, via text you can "Flext" (quickly flex or change the time/date of a meeting or ask your daughter to start the dishwasher or clean up her room). Second, you can also "Connext" (send a daily greeting and words of praise to your girl), and finally, you can "Rxt" (text her to get her over a rough spot or uplift her or help her solve her problems).

If you steadfastly disagree with your daughter, write an explanation about why you feel the way you do and give it to her. Give reasons from your life. Or draw a picture of yourself looking dejected with the caption, "Please help me understand." Or text her a picture of the two of you having lunch while on a shopping trip with the caption, "When can we do that again?" Your hope is that during the next outing, you two will hash out what stands in the way. Do whatever you can to get your daughter to open up to you. You know that you and she speak the same language even though she may not know it yet.

NOTE TO MOM

Encourage your daughter to communicate with you in various ways whether she is upset with you or not. She can scribble you a note when she is mad or sad. This can be her "pass," similar to a bathroom pass her teacher hands out. Use the note over and over as a quick reminder that it is time for both of you to sit down and talk. Vary the talk stations. Talk to your girl at a place and time of her choosing. Sometimes while doing the dinner preparations or before a tricky situation develops works best. You may find that a less direct talk works well, such as when you are on a walk, in the car, or doing an activity together. This is a great way to pause any emotionally intense situations as well.

A Friend or a Mother?

The relationship between a mother and a daughter should never be an either/or situation, as in "Is my mother my friend or my mother?" You are both. As such, you realize that from the beginning of time, girls have told their mothers when they disagreed with them, "You just don't understand me." Tempered with patience and a willingness to see your daughter's side, you can be a great mom if you just hang in there during your daughter's ups and downs, and offer encouragement whenever needed.

Mothers often try to be as understanding and supportive as their daughters' best friends. That is not quite possible because a mother's wisdom and experience overarches the friendly feelings, thereby giving her the ability to sense or see obstacles on the horizon long before her daughter has an inkling. Instead, strive to be both a motherly friend and a friendly mother, rather than solely your daughter's "best friend." If you err on the side of treating your daughter like a friend, you will see pushback when you kick into mom-mode and start setting limits and boundaries. Who wants their best friend telling them what to do? You need to retain a balance, being warm and friendly and yet still firm when needed.

Why Nothing Moms Do Is Right

Sometimes it seems as if nothing you do is right from your daughter's point of view. In this case, just be confident that those days will pass, too. Try not to take it personally. What can help is having a good relationship with yourself, so you do not rise or fall with the emotional roller-coaster ride your daughter will have to take—sooner or later—to grow into the fine young woman she will eventually become.

If you are a mother of a girl who suddenly is very critical of you, realize that she is maturing. While examining some characteristics in you—some of which she may see emerging in herself—she may be surprised. Criticism of a mother is a girl's attempt to find traits to adore and adopt. In a way, this is a flattering development. If she did not care, she would simply overlook you.

BEING DETHRONED

Do you remember the day your mother fell off her pedestal? Suddenly one day you saw her as the most out-of-touch frump in the world. Even her best shoes made you shudder. Yet a few years later, you changed your opinion of her drastically. As you hit your twenties, you saw her again the way you did at age eight or nine—as the best mom in the whole world.

It is only natural in the creation of a strong mother-daughter bond that tension will occur to test the threads that make up the bond. That tension helps your connection with your girl prevail through any temporary kinks or knots. You may find it difficult to see yourself dethroned overnight, but try to feel some relief as well. You can be a real person now, not someone so elevated in your daughter's eyes that you fear making a mistake.

BEING HUMAN

Trust that you will make mistakes, and not only as a mother. You are human, and as your daughter changes, so do you. Get out your old year-books and prove it. Show her pictures of yourself with bad hair and geeky outfits. Laugh with her over your first dance dress and your first date. Do not be surprised if your daughter acts like a chameleon. One day she giggles with you and sees your point; the next she gives you that look that disdainfully says, "Mom!" Just remember that you have years of experience as a parent, and it is your job to keep your eyes on the big picture. Often the more volatile your relationship with your daughter is at times, the better it will turn out to be when she is older.

Give her a little extra TLC whenever she makes you feel you cannot please her:

O Put a surprise present—small and just right—on her pillow.

O Give her a funny card.

O Text her a picture of something that reminds you of her.

O Give her a diary with a big lock and key and tell her to use it to "spill her guts."

O Surprise her with a special outing with just you and her. It can be as simple as her picking a favorite restaurant to go to together or a "girls' weekend" somewhere.

Count on this: Confrontations, accusations, and emotional outbursts from your daughter show that you are on the right track. Often it all depends on your and her personality types. Some mothers and daughters show little friction in their relationship; others have a run-in every other week. But how can you expand your parenting skills if you are not confronted with new challenges?

If your daughter keeps telling you that she hates you, tell her how that makes you feel, without overreacting. Tell her that your feelings are hurt and you will talk about what is bothering her later. In the heat of the moment, you could say things you don't want to say, as could she. When she has calmed down, ask her why she hates you, acknowledge her feelings, and do what you can to mitigate the conflict. Most importantly, tell her you love her enough for both of you.

Think of raising your girl as a most wonderful adventure. Certainly there will be a few or quite a few nerve-racking moments. Otherwise it would not be an adventure. So assume that the generations will clash now and then at your house, and be ready for it. Call it the pangs of your daughter becoming herself.

Being Cool with Your Daughter

One of the biggest challenges many mothers face is accepting their daughters as they truly are. Why? Because sometimes it seems like the universe is in a joking mood. Many former-tomboy moms get real girly girls, and vice versa. Many social-butterfly mothers get daughters who are shy and like to bury their noses in books. This appears to be the result of a generational pendulum that is invisible. A majority of mothers indeed end up with daughters who are their opposites in personality, preferences, and pastimes.

If you make your life a little happier, you will make your daughter's life a little happier, too. You cannot be a good mother unless you are good to yourself first. You know that as a mother you can easily get overextended, so be sure to make room in your life for some free and fun times for yourself—and your girl.

A SPECIAL RELATIONSHIP

The more your daughter tests your parenting limits, the more she makes you expand your abilities. You will feel special because you have a special girl. Should there be a moment when you feel like throwing up your hands in frustration because you may see in your daughter the precursors of mistakes you made in your youth, enjoy the moment. How? By focusing not on the negatives from which your frustration sprang, but by enjoying your daughter more. Remember, a daughter positively affects her mother just as much as a mother positively affects her daughter. Raising a girl is an important task and one that benefits you by giving you the chance to:

O Grow and become a better person because you realize how important setting a good example is.

O Repeat and relive the highlights of your life because you can share your daughter's special occasions, graduations, and award ceremonies.

O Stay young in outlook and even physically because you can experience firsthand the younger generation.

O See your daughter come into her own, whether she shares your traits or not, and appreciate her uniqueness and individuality.

For these reasons, make sure your relationship with your daughter is strong. That requires a back-and-forth connection that is vibrant. Being a conscious parent means stepping back and hovering above your parent-child interactions instead of falling into a default-mode of parenting of barking orders. You have an opportunity to choose the positive traits from your own parents and change the ones that were not optimal. When you stop to consider the choices you can make to support your relationship, and parent with purpose, you are setting the stage for positive interactions with your daughter.

Bonding Activities

Mothers and daughters can have more fun than other twosomes because they have a common history, tend to think alike, and may have many similar passions. Find out what your girl gets excited about and share in her excitement. There are so many opportunities for you two to do that. You can discuss with her turning your household "greener" by stepping up your recycling, reusing, and donating efforts. You can go shopping together at the grocery store, antique shops, and flea markets. You can stretch, work out, run, or walk the dog together. Afterward you can eat out, or search through cookbooks and try cooking the most mouthwatering dishes. You can splurge and head for a day spa for mother-daughter manicures and pedicures, or do housework together until you are ready to drop. You could treat each other to a sauna and sweat buckets like marathon runners, dip into the ice-cold dunking pool together, or have a relaxing massage.

Just ask your daughter what would make her happy and incorporate her wishes into your week, month, or vacation time as much as you can. Zero in on her interests and yours. If they are not compatible, follow your heart's desires as individuals, then meet up and talk about what each of you did, saw, and experienced. Every day work on that wonderful bond you have with your girl. It takes a little effort, sure, but how nice that you have the chance to do it. Fashion the bond with your best intentions and efforts, and the sweat of your brow and your soul. Give your girl all the goodness in you that you can muster.

Keep in mind that the happiest times for you and your daughter come from being active or going through a process together. Short-term happiness can come from "things" you can buy for your daughter, but long-term sustainable happiness comes from experiences shared together.

SKILLS FOR CONNECTING WITH YOUR DAUGHTER

A daughter's bond with her mother is one of the deepest, most enduring relationships she will experience in her lifetime. It should also be one of the healthiest and most supportive. Here are some suggestions for building a strong, loving connection with your girl:

- **Listen and observe.** Good mothers are willing to spend time just listening and watching. Ask "what" and "how" questions to draw out your daughter. Let her finish her thoughts before offering suggestions or advice.

- **Spend time just being together.** Relationships require time. You must be willing to hang out, play, and do things face-to-face with your daughter. Have at least fifteen minutes a day that belong just to your daughter. Put aside your cell phone, have your other children (if you have them) engaged in something else, and just *be* with your daughter—fully present, free from distractions, and engaged in her world.

○ **Respond to your daughter's cues.** When she says, "I can do it my-self, Mom!" teach the necessary skills, be sure she's safe, and allow her to try. Skills and experience build self-esteem.

○ **Be curious about her interests.** If your daughter loves an activity, sharing her enthusiasm is a wonderful way to build connection. Watch her favorite sport with her; admire the new pair of jeans she bought or the new painting she made. Understanding your daughter's world will keep you connected.

○ **Know her friends.** There is no better way to learn about your daughter than to watch her at play with her friends. As your daughter grows, welcome her friends into your home. If she can bring her life to you, she is less likely to feel the need to hide it from you.

○ **Respect her privacy.** Even little girls need time to themselves. Your daughter may choose to play alone in her room from time to time, or to disappear into her computer games or headphones to listen to music. You can show her that you care and still respect her need for private space.

○ **Provide kind, firm discipline and don't be afraid to follow through.** "Wait till your father gets home" doesn't work. Learn effective discipline skills; then be willing to set limits and follow through.

○ **Be sensitive about touch, especially in public.** Hugs are wonderful, but sometimes public affection may make your daughter un-comfortable, especially in the later tween years when her friends may tease her if they see her being openly affectionate toward you. Respecting her needs will keep the connection between you relaxed and open.

Girls need connection with their mothers. Your knowledge of your daughter will help you recognize when she welcomes a hug and when she does not. It is a delicate balancing act, but time and love will teach you how to stay connected to your daughter at the same time that you encourage her to exercise her independence.

MOM AS A FOUNDATION

Think far ahead as you parent your daughter. Consider her in the years to come and how—in all likelihood—she may experience some pain, tragedy, and heartbreak. It is inevitable that she will face her share of losses. Even you may not be able to prevent them from happening to your daughter at some point in her life. But you can ease her disappointments and dim, divert, or alert her about many of them. Be sure to give your girl the certainty that whatever happens, the two of you can deal with it.

Be strong and solid as a rock for your daughter, and help alleviate her worst times by being her supporter. In return, you will feel empowered that you were able to pass on to her the gift of your strength. You want so much for your daughter to grow up to be independent, strong willed, and kind. Help her on her way with empowerment, energy, and endless love.

Important Points to Consider

The mother-daughter bond is one that has a natural ebb and flow. Some moments are full and rich with love and friendship and others are full of conflict. But there is no doubt that a mother and daughter share an important connection, and you can help promote a positive one by keeping the following in mind:

O Not all mother-daughter relationships are marked by frequent clashes. It often depends on your and your daughter's personalities. Your daughter's may be similar or different from yours. If it is different, seek understanding rather than trying to change who she is.

○ Confrontations, accusations, and emotional outbursts from your daughter are to be expected, and they show that you are on the right track. See these moments as an opportunity for you to expand your conscious parenting skills.

○ The way we talk to our daughters becomes their inner voice. No mother is perfect and able to convey all positive messages all the time, so be forgiving. If you find yourself saying something to your daughter in the heat of the moment that was harsher than you wanted, take ownership and apologize to her. This teaches her to do the same.

○ Use technology to keep lines of communication open. Sending e-mails and texts to your daughter when things are going smoothly as well as when you are in a tough spot with your relationship can help you connect (or reconnect) with your girl.

CHAPTER 12

Self-Esteem

Many problems young girls face are attributed to a lack of self-esteem, from low achievement and depression to a rise in teen pregnancy, drug use, and crime involvement. Unfortunately, you as a parent cannot give your daughter self-esteem; its roots already lie within her. What you can do is acknowledge and celebrate who she is and teach her to be proud of her accomplishments. Remember to lead by example and show your daughter what it is like to be a confident person. Armed with proper knowledge and unyielding determination, you can create a home climate conducive to boosting your girl's self-esteem.

Images of Women and the Media

The main reason for a girl's low self-esteem is the reflections of women she sees in the media, the stores, and the movies. Wherever she glances, she sees images of females that are completely unrealistic. They are presented to her as ideals to emulate while being out of her reach. No matter how much your daughter strives to be just like them, she cannot achieve the extreme thinness, height, and photogenic facial structures. For that reason, the constant barrage of messages about what your daughter ought to look like can erode her confidence and lower her self-esteem.

But do not worry. The false images that flood your daughter's field of vision cannot stand up to the real images of females you present to your daughter. You know you can get a handle on this issue. You can make sure she meets real women who do great things, and you can stress to her that real women come in all sizes.

One popular definition of *self-esteem* is self-worth. Psychologically speaking, this is a human being's self-image at an emotional level and has nothing to do with logical thinking or reasoning. Some experts define *self-esteem* as self-respect or a feeling of confidence in one's own merit.

MASTER THE MYTHS

You know how detrimental it would be if someone told your girl every day that she does not measure up and never will. So you are not about to permit her to receive similar negative messages without first teaching her to separate fact from fantasy. It is time for her to master the myths about female appearance that millions of girls still buy into.

Most women shown by the media are fantasy creations. There is very little reality to them. Explain the airbrushing techniques used in photo shoots and layouts to your girl. Explain all the lengthy preparations it takes to get ready for just one picture, like the hassle of the hairdo, the stiff and aching muscles that result from hours of staying put in one position, the team of lighting and styling professionals, and the layers of heavy makeup put on models' faces.

It is important that you take every opportunity to teach your daughter the following quick facts:

O Everybody is born with a different body and all body types are great.

O A healthy body is more important than a "good-looking" body. Many actresses and models have unhealthy eating practices to retain their figures, which can be detrimental to their overall health.

O Models and many movie stars have genes that make them tall and thin, and they spend most of their days working out to keep thin. They also spend lots of time dieting and focusing on their clothes and appearances.

O Since looks last only a short time, models and movie stars often have short prime periods and often end up looking for other work.

Stress to your daughter that it is dangerous to compare herself to famous people because she does not know them personally and cannot know their reasons for living and working the way they do. Also remind her that appearances can be deceiving; even the thinnest, tallest, and best-photographed young women may have low self-esteem because every year there is another huge crop of gorgeous newcomers in their field. Models and actresses are constantly in danger of being replaced. For them, fame is definitely fleeting.

Once you have added some reality to today's fabricated media images of women, you want to use some sure-fire self-esteem builders with your daughter. Begin with yourself. Be comfortable and happy with your looks. Don't make negative comments about your body in front of your daughter. Wear a swimsuit even if you don't have a perfect figure. She'll remember fondly playing with you in the ocean or pool, not worrying one bit if your tummy was sticking out a bit. Never compare your daughter to the screen versions. Know you are the most influential person in the growth of your daughter's self-confidence.

TOY TEST

Take a look at your girl's toys and games to make sure they are not detrimental to her self-worth. Many playthings marketed to girls these days, such as certain brands of dolls, contain secret self-esteem-damaging messages. One of them is that your daughter is only valuable as a beauty-conscious and fashion-aware consumer.

Do not buy a product from a company that runs ads that make girls feel bad about themselves. Also, do not let your daughter buy magazines or read blogs that make her feel less confident. Why should you, or she, support any business that makes her feel worse about herself?

What you want to do is make your daughter more critical of the messages she receives about girls. Teach her to critique what she sees and to always be proud of her body and who she is. She is no one's object to be manipulated, duped, or used. No one can make her feel inferior, according to Eleanor Roosevelt, without her consent.

Your daughter must know how wonderful she is. She is more precious than any possession—a special young person with so many options, talents, and important tasks ahead.

Tell your girl that sometimes magazines can be like upscale clothing stores for her to browse through and to enjoy. They can give her some idea of what styles and outfits might be flattering on her, now and later. But teach her to be a critical consumer by pointing out that the one photo of a girl frolicking on the beach probably took a whole day and a team of professionals to make look perfect and this is unrealistic. Also make sure she has plenty of other reading materials on hand, including magazines about other interests, such as hobbies, sports, cooking, travel, or whatever else she may be interested in.

Am I Pretty?

With so many false images crowding in on her, is it any wonder that your daughter asks, "Am I pretty?" or "Don't I look pretty?" when donning her new dress? It is naïve to think that looks do not matter at all. Attractive people are often perceived as more capable, smarter, and more interesting in our society. Your daughter will get plenty of compliments about her looks out there in the world. Your job is to give her a broader perspective—her inner qualities are even more important than her outer package. Retool your comments about her looks to include what makes her pretty in a larger context: her warm smile, her bright and curious eyes, her strong and healthy body ready for taking on the world.

Instead of only commenting on what she is wearing, comment on her excellent sense of style or her ability to pick a great outfit that she can be comfortable and free to play in. You don't have to hold your tongue and refrain from all comments about appearance, but spend time emphasizing the message that she is more than just how she looks.

See to it that your daughter does not obsess over her looks and allow her body to become her pet project by which she measures herself. The problem is that many girls have an "ugly duckling" imprint on their minds because when they first started peering at themselves in the mirror—at age nine, ten, or eleven—they may have been at an awkward stage in their lives, as far as their looks are concerned. Due to "before and after" product ads bombarding them, your daughter may see buying the "right" products as the key to her transformation into a beautiful swan. Again, you can help her understand that while looks are important in our society, character matters more.

In reality, bodily dissatisfaction is prevalent in teens. One study by the National Institute on Medial and the Family reports that at age thirteen, 53 percent of American girls are "unhappy with their bodies." This grows to 78 percent by the time a girl reaches seventeen.

For that reason, make sure your daughter is happy with hers. Skip any empty, overused words and instead compliment her about her healthy body and all the good things she accomplishes with it, such as helping you around the house and excelling on the track team.

WORST MOMENT

Just like an image becomes imprinted on film, too many girls take a mental snapshot of themselves at a time when their bodies are still child-like and their teeth are misaligned, or when they have gangly arms and legs and have not yet grown to their adult height and shape. Then they cling to that snapshot like a road map to a hidden treasure and never let go of it. This mistaken imprint sets them up for a life of body discontent.

Instill in your daughter the idea that women (and men) are so much more than their appearance. It is better to measure people by what they accomplish and the good they do, rather than by what they look like. Did it matter what Mother Teresa or Marie Curie looked like? It is your girl's brains and bravery that will take her far. Encourage her friendships with girls and boys who possess these traits and have the qualities of drive and determination in common with your daughter.

BEST MOVE

Of course your daughter's self-esteem will ebb and flow, like the tides. One day she will be supremely confident because she just made an A in algebra. The next day she will feel less sure of herself because she was not prepared for a Spanish pop quiz. Tell her to accept the fluctuations of her self-esteem. Show her you always esteem her unwaveringly. Prove to her that you like her company, and include her friends if you can, but do not coddle her. Let her experience failure sometimes. Redoubling her efforts the next time will make her stronger.

A companion to self-esteem is self-compassion, which is not striving to be the best in comparison to others but being loving and kind toward oneself, faults and all. In essence, instead of judging ourselves harshly, we give ourselves the same caring support that we would give a friend. The research of Dr. Kristin Neff and others shows that such self-compassion gives people feelings of security and self-worth. Further, when we fail or get hurt, self-compassion is a tool that helps us get back up again and lead a productive life.

Popularity

When it comes to making a difference for others, big accomplishments can have lasting and glorious effects, while just going for popularity may bring in nothing more than a few cents. However, girls from middle school on can become too concerned with popularity. They notice a girl being admired by her clique for her looks, the way she acts, or her material possessions and are dying to get more attention, too.

With the proliferation of smartphones, some girls now think their popularity rises with the number of texts they receive or the amount of "likes" they get on their social media feeds. This development causes girls who get only a few messages to do a dumb thing: They post sexually revealing pictures of themselves on Facebook, post something hurtful about another person, or send out a sext in hopes of getting more attention. They do get a result, but not the kind they want.

> Remind your daughter that a digital footprint lasts forever and one inappropriate or suggestive picture can be sent to every single person in her school (and even all over the world) in a matter of minutes. To illustrate this, Google yourself in front of your daughter and show her all the images of you that you and others have posted over the years.

MISSING PURPOSE

Most girls who are swept away by the allure of popularity and become preoccupied with the approval of their peers are missing an important concept that can stabilize them even during uncertain times. The therapist and writer Mary Pipher calls this a girl's "North Star." Other experts call it her "anchor," "focus," or "center." Whatever name is attached to this concept that guides a girl is unimportant. What is important is that your daughter has a core interest, a passion, a love for something that truly excites her. It may be her involvement with sculling or the Girl Scouts. It may be studying the effects of global warming in her backyard or starting a paperback give-away program with her English class.

MISSION ACCOMPLISHED

Whatever your daughter has settled on as her centering activity, stand behind her and support her in a conscious, loving way. The power of popularity and the urge to fit in with the popular crowd at her school will wane when your daughter has something in her life that is much more important to her. Trust her not to be blinded for long by girls who are still searching for a purpose in their teenage lives and by that clique swarming around them. She will eventually understand that these girls are attempting to feel good about themselves by finding safety in numbers.

Fads and Trends

Fads and trends can be fun for your daughter when they are not overdone. By definition, fads enjoy a brief popularity. In other words, they come and go. They can add spice to your girl's life if she knows how to handle them and put them into their proper perspective. Fads and trends generally express themselves in these areas:

- O Fashions

- O Collectibles

- O Activities

- O Events

Fads can be harmless, adding color to her otherwise blah days, or they can be harmful, have repercussions, and leave lasting scars. Any fad relating to your girl's health needs looking into. If there is a latest diet craze (eat only what the cavemen ate; drink only green juice for a week) or something that is trickling down to your daughter's lunchroom, talk about it with her, and specifically discuss the dangers of following trends blindly. In talking to your daughter, point out some of the foolish trends of the past decades. Each had one major "craze," or several.

Clothing, Style, and Makeup

Your daughter can have the whole world at her fingertips in her choice of clothing, style, and makeup long before she really has the whole world at her fingertips in her choice of college, career, and lifestyle. Unlike with boys' clothing, girls have a huge menu of modes to explore. They can gravitate toward the preppie look, the boho (bohemian) style, sports apparel, classic clothes—whatever they think expresses their personalities best. And they do not have to get stuck with one designer look or line.

FASHION VANE

Your daughter can change as frequently in her preferences of clothes, purses, and shoes as a weather vane. She can dabble in makeup and hair ornaments. While boys' gear usually sticks to the same colors and styles and varies little from year to year, girls have at their disposal a whole gamut of hues and fashions. No other segment of society has more apparel options than your daughter and her girlfriends. Use this fact as an opportunity for your girl to:

O Explore the designs she likes.

O Develop new fashion interests.

O Celebrate her creativity and sense of color.

O Be daring in trying new looks.

This way, the world of style is just a forerunner to the real world. At the makeup counter, the sales shelves, and the shoe racks, she can practice making good, informed choices. This quality will serve her well for the rest of her life. So by all means, if your girl's budget allows it and you approve, let her get the latest hot sunglasses or glittery eye shadow.

Talk with her about what messages other items convey, like T-shirts with offensive words on them or age-inappropriate cuts. You will not have total control over what she wears, nor should you. But you do control the purse strings for quite a while and can guide her along the way. Once she makes her own money, she may step out of your comfort zone, but this is natural and you want your daughter to develop her own style. But do not overlook passing on to your daughter the real secrets of timeless style: poise and personality. They will always be her best assets and cost nothing. There's no sense in being the best-dressed girl with a horrible attitude, unless your goal is to alienate yourself from others.

When it comes to your girl's emerging style, relax. Her desire to have her way of being and doing things is universal among growing girls. Do not let it interfere with your relationship. There is never a need to pressure your daughter about her outfits, as long as they are not offensive. Some girls simply do not give a flip about fancy labels; good for you if your daughter is one of them. It saves money, plus it shows that she is ahead of other girls who act as though they cannot go to school unless they are wearing the latest style, which may look a lot like what you or your sister wore when you were their age. There are only so many styles, so of course a lot of them are recycled—and more than once.

Current Culture

Ever since the early 1960s, the term *popular culture*, or *pop culture*, has been on many people's lips. It refers to the modern lifestyle that finds its expression in fashion, music, sports, movies, and the media. For your daughter to get a grip on it, inform her that she and her generation are the engine that drives the latest culture, and not the other way around.

For that reason, imitating current culture or keeping up with it is beneficial when it adds something positive to her day. But when it detracts from her healthy development and growth, she should avoid it. Current culture has tried unsuccessfully to pigeonhole women. Your daughter's beauty is not related to her shape, size, or style. Those vary from one girl to the next and matter little, overall.

GIRL POWER

Young women are wonderful people who should make waves, work on fulfilling their wishes, widen their scope as much as possible, and try to right wrongs. They are not mindless things, walking clothes racks, sales inducements, objects, or adornments. Make sure your daughter understands this and does not allow other girls, or pop culture, to define who she is.

As a conscious parent, you are striving to teach her to follow her inner compass. She does not have to be all things, all the time. The "girl power" movement has its merits, but she should not have to feel pressure to be beautiful but not conceited, smart but humble, poised but not afraid to show flaws, multi-talented and super strong in one activity, fierce and assertive, kind and collaborative—essentially all great traits at all times. This is a tall order for anyone! She just needs to be herself, and you can embrace her core—with all its triumphs and faults. Just like adult women sometimes struggle with being "supermoms" who do it all, your daughter might be faced with pressure to be too many things at once. You want to send a message that she does not have to do it all. Part of being a girl, and a human for that matter, is being imperfect and accepting of yourself, as you are.

Mary Pipher, author of the bestselling book *Reviving Ophelia: Saving the Selves of Adolescent Girls*, coined the term *girl-poisoning culture* and explained the damage it can do. She offers parents strategies for overcoming the negative effects that might show up in their daughters.

Every day the way you look at and talk to your daughter helps her become stronger and more capable. When you greet her with joy and encouragement in your eyes, and a few well-chosen, warm words, you add to her outer and inner armor. Make it powerful so it can withstand any onslaught from whatever cultural currents might come rushing her way.

Important Points to Consider

Your daughter's self-esteem is shaped by the messages she receives. You will want to be the strongest voice in her developing self-worth, by educating her on unhealthy messages that she should discard. While you cannot shield her from the media and popular culture, you can be a voice of reason in her life. Keep the following in mind as you develop your conscious parenting skills and your daughter's own awareness about self-esteem:

O Self-esteem is not only one thing. Your daughter can have strong self-esteem in various areas of her life, in her appearance, achievements, relationships, and interests.

O Bear in mind that popular culture and the media tend to be heavy handed in only one area of self-esteem for girls: their looks. Teach media literacy and make your daughter aware of media manipulation. You can't change the way fashion models look, but you can teach your daughter that a team of professionals was required to achieve her look.

O Have empathy for your daughter as she grapples with her looks and expectations for beauty and keeping up with the latest trends. It is easy for parents to say, "Looks don't matter as much as your personality," but your daughter is getting a slew of messages to the contrary. Stay steadfast in your message while appreciating and empathizing with her experience.

O Appreciate your daughter's emerging sense of style and try not to micromanage her choices. Clothing and trends are ways for her to express herself.

O Keep in mind that you want to strike a balance between instilling self-esteem in your daughter and avoiding inadvertently teaching her self-obsession and entitlement. Help her find her core—her "North Star"—of confidence without being perfect or the best at everything.

 **CHAPTER 13**

Dangers and Warning Signs

In addition to the overabundance of girl-demeaning messages that permeate society, many other dangers can lurk in the wings for your daughter. These dangers may be posed by her environment, her peer group, or the opposite sex, or they may be of her own making. But take heart. All these dangers send up red flags. Therefore, all you have to do is be on the lookout for them, and then deal with any potentially perilous situation. Remember not to overreact if any of these red flags pop up. Try to remain calm and approach the situation with perspective and grace.

Drinking, Smoking, and Drugs

The most obvious dangers your girl can face may come from drinking, smoking, and drugs. All three of these activities are in evidence everywhere. From sixth grade on or earlier, some of her classmates will probably experiment with them.

DAUGHTER DANGERS

While illicit drug use among adolescents is on the decline, according to a 2015 study by National Institute on Drug Abuse, and while teenage boys used to try alcohol, cigarettes, and drugs at a higher rate than girls, the reverse is now true. This puts your daughter in a precarious situation because most people believe girls are at a lesser risk. Therefore, they concentrate on helping boys refrain from using harmful substances.

By focusing mostly on boys, people neglect the girls who need our attention as well. Unfortunately you cannot rid your girl's school or community of these dangers, but rest assured that you do have power when it comes to your girl and dangerous substances. You definitely play the most important part in helping your girl to resist any drug- or alcohol-related temptations she may come across.

SAFE DAUGHTER

According to Dr. Ralph Lopez, who specializes in adolescent medicine, girls are more at risk for drug and alcohol abuse than boys because they are under more stress—the stress of succeeding academically and of looking perfect. In contrast, boys do not face that double pressure.

Know that with your parenting skills ratcheted up into high gear, you can tackle anything that threatens your girl. You are tough—good for you. As a result, you welcome the chance to educate yourself about how best to protect your girl from the scourge of illegal drug use. This is especially important because not only are girls more vulnerable to the lures of drinking, smoking, and drugs than boys, but they can also suffer worse consequences than boys:

O Girls may become addicted to nicotine more quickly than boys.

○ Even moderate drinking can interrupt girls' normal growth patterns.

○ Drugs may also interfere with the development of female reproductive systems.

Fortunately, you have been talking to your daughter about the dangers of cigarettes, drinking, and drugs from first grade on. If not, now is the time to start having a serious conversation—parent to daughter—about these topics and to keep the conversation going. Tell your girl about the high expectations you have for her. Tell her you understand the challenges of saying no to temptations, and prepare her for how to handle situations. It's not a shady figure in an alley coaxing your daughter to try drugs. It's often her closest friends, which can create a social bind for her.

When it comes to nicotine, drugs, and alcohol, parents should never try to be popular with their daughter and her friends and allow them to drink a beer or a glass of wine or smoke a cigarette at home. Parents may think they are doing the teenagers a favor. In reality they are teaching them to break the law.

The sooner you let your girl know exactly where you stand in regard to the use of alcohol and drugs, the better. This begins with you serving as her role model. Your personal conduct vis-à-vis these substances will reinforce your heart-to-heart talks. One without the other will ring hollow. If parents cannot control their conduct with nicotine, booze, and illegal (or prescription) drugs, how can they expect their daughter to control hers? Also, arm yourself with knowledge so that you can recognize the warning signs of your daughter's dabbling with these dangerous substances.

GIRLS DRINKING

Take care not to get overly suspicious about your girl's every move and gesture. Often just plain growing pains are the reason that your daughter's behavior is a little worrisome now and then. But when you notice her acting strangely over and over, and when you have a sinking feeling about her behavior, you should investigate if she and her friends have started drinking. Be on the lookout for the following signs that may indicate your daughter is beginning to experiment with alcohol:

- Suddenly switching to a new group of friends and not wanting you to meet them

- A "who cares" attitude coupled with neglecting her former interests and her appearance

- Finding alcohol in her room or smelling it on her breath

- Bloodshot eyes, slurred speech, and a lack of coordination

If your daughter exhibits any of these signs, she is calling out for help. This is when you have to put everything else aside, sit down with her, and find out what is going on. Communication and support are key in this situation.

Do not sweep your uneasy feelings about what you think you have observed in your daughter under the rug. Since alcohol is forbidden until age twenty-one in the United States, teenagers here see it as more enticing than those in countries where the age limit is lower. Therefore, most parties that your daughter and her friends attend will probably have opportunities to drink. Talk to your girl before she heads out to one of those parties. Tell her you are concerned about her welfare and safety. Warn her about the possibility of the punch being spiked and prepare her for what to say if someone offers her an alcoholic drink. Most likely, her very own friends will be the ones offering her alcohol. Arm her with things to say that can get her off the hook with her peers, such as, "No thanks, I have a game tomorrow and I need to be at my best," "No thanks, I'm taking it easy tonight," or when she is older, "I'm the designated driver tonight." She can also practice plain old assertiveness: "I'm not really a drinker."

You will also want to have a frank conversation with her about what to do if she or her friends do decide to drink. Set up a "no punishment" agreement that if she or others have been drinking and need a ride home, you will come get them or pay for a ride without punishing her. You don't want her driving or getting in a car with someone who has been drinking for fear of punishment.

It is much easier to root out the beginnings of a teenage drinking problem before it sets in. The same is true for your girl's attraction to smoking.

GIRLS SMOKING

To many parents, cigarette smoking seems like a lesser evil compared to drinking and drugs. They know that about a quarter of all adolescents smoke, or have tried it, so they are not too worried. Besides, some parents smoke themselves.

Girls whose parents smoke are much more likely to start smoking themselves than girls whose parents do not smoke. Not only are these girls more used to the sights and smells of smokers, but they also are able to help themselves to their parents' pack of cigarettes without any trouble and without having to pay for them.

But what some parents tend to overlook is the fact that nicotine is addictive. Once your daughter picks up the habit, it may be hard for her to quit. Smoking cigarettes may also be the first step toward smoking marijuana, so watch out for these warning signs in your girl:

○ Using air freshener or perfume to minimize the smell of tobacco

○ Hanging out with a crowd of known smokers

○ Always needing money, yet having nothing to show for it, such as a new purchase

○ Your own cigarettes disappearing at a faster rate than usual

Make it very clear to your daughter that you do not want her to smoke. Tell her that, according to the Center for Disease Control, smoking is very likely to cause Chronic Obstructive Pulmonary Disease (COPD), and it accounts for as many as eight out of 10 COPD-related deaths. Also, about one-third of all smokers will develop a serious smoke-related disease such as emphysema or lung cancer.

You can also emphasize more immediate consequences that matter to teens, such as yellow teeth, smelling bad, poorer athletic performance, and all her money she might want to spend on other things being siphoned off by cigarettes. She may not seem to pay attention to your lecture, but some of it will stick with her—count on it. That may mean you have to stop smoking in front of her, if you do. You do not want your girl to look at you with pity every time you light up, or think you are not as strong as she thought you were.

GIRLS DOING DRUGS

Just as some teens your daughter befriends will start drinking and smoking long before it is legal, some of them also will be enticed by the drug world. Especially in high school, your girl may become exposed to adolescents who use the whole campus as their drug-dealing domain. Warn her to be wary of any teenager who possesses huge amounts of cash. Also ask her to stay away from adolescents who find the drug culture "cool." Yet even if you could patrol the halls of your girl's school personally, some of her classmates would still manage to offer her illegal substances. Not all adolescents have parents who supervise them properly. Therefore, even in the best schools a few teenagers may start dealing drugs, or start producing them in a lab somewhere. "Meth is almost like a body snatcher. It reaches out and grabs these kids almost overnight," warns Dr. Jim Lewis, a school district superintendent.

You also want to caution your girl against using prescription drugs without a prescription. Teens may have a false sense that they are safer because a doctor prescribed them, but they can be unsafe when taken by someone else.

In regard to marijuana, since it is now legal in several states, your conversation about using it will be more similar to your conversations about alcohol than those about illegal drugs. However, it is still a controlled substance until a certain age, and just because something is legal doesn't necessarily make it healthy. Educate her on the risks, both short- and long-term.

Be on the alert for these warning signs that may indicate that your daughter could be experimenting with drugs:

O Exhibiting secretive conduct and frequent irritability

O Seeming to be dizzy, staying up late, and losing weight

O Being unusually silly and giggling for no reason

O Having red, bloodshot eyes and acting differently than usual

Some of these signs relate to using marijuana; others are red flags for additional drugs.

It definitely pays to be aware of any abrupt changes in your daughter and also to notice other symptoms of drug use in her, such as unusual tiredness, listlessness and depression, worsening relationships with long-time friends and close family members, and—of course—the appearance of drug paraphernalia.

Don't wait until your daughter asks about your experience with drugs. During your next serious talk, depending on your daughter's age, tell her honestly about some of the mistakes you made when you were young and how you have regretted them. It's better to be honest about the appeal of drugs and the consequences than to only talk about the dangers. Going over-board and emphasizing only the dangers may not resonate with her, because she probably has friends who have experimented and had nothing catastrophic happen. Talk about the research on long-term negative effects. Stress that overlooking the latest research is not the thing for a smart girl like your daughter to do.

Besides identifying and worrying about a daughter's alcohol, cigarette, and illegal drug use, parents of girls in particular have another headache these days. They have to be less concerned with traditional drugs and more with drugs that are very easy to obtain and hide. What is worse, most girls do not even consider them drugs because these are legally prescribed medications.

"PHARM" PARTIES

The latest rage among many kids is holding "pharm" parties, or get-togethers where pharmaceuticals are passed around like potato chips. Girls are especially susceptible to participation in these parties because they require—as admission tickets—nothing more than a handful of their parents' medicines that the parents will surely never miss. There is no dealing with any shady characters in a pharm party, so they seem to have a more innocent feel to the girls involved. The girls who attend are typically from nice homes and similar neighborhoods, so there is a false sense of safety. Your daughter may think, "What's wrong with popping a pink or purple pill, or two?"

What the girls who go to pharm parties do not realize is that many drugs are incompatible. Besides, taking drugs meant for an ailment can make a healthy girl sick. Plus, there is always the chance of overdosing, which can lead to death. Therefore, you must be on the lookout for these warning signs that may indicate your daughter is engaged in pharming:

○ Your old medicines are disappearing.

○ Your current medicines are running out faster than they should.

○ It looks as if someone has gone through your medicine cabinet.

○ Your daughter is suddenly very curious about all your prescriptions.

○ Your daughter has someone else's medicine in her purse or pockets.

In regard to your daughter and her friends getting into your medications and maybe even passing them out to other teens, you cannot stick your head in the sand. You need to talk frankly with your girl about the dangers of legal and illegal drug use. If she is showing any warning signs of use, you should keep prescription drugs in a place where they are not easily accessible. Your number-one goal is prevention. Your girl's health is precious and she must not compromise it. Furthermore, her reputation is fragile. It will follow her wherever she goes. So she must make a point of staying away from kids who have the mindset of "I'll try anything once, or twice." What can make kids like these so dangerous is that your daughter may be attracted to some of them because she thinks they are "cute" and overlook the unhealthy choices they are making.

Abusive Boys

Your daughter may dream of holding hands with a cute boy her age, but instead she may end up with a bruise. Why? Because some boys—having no positive role models at home—may grow up to be controlling and abusive in their relationships.

Your daughter's friendship with a boy may not start out being violent. It may begin with a little jealousy, then go on to too many texts that are demanding and controlling. While at first she might be pleased to get so many messages from a boy, soon the over-texting may take on a threatening tone. Next may come threats and physical blows, or worse. Warn your daughter about the possibility of dating violence and teach her how to spot warning signs of a potentially violent relationship. These days, many are related to texting, such as receiving too many texts from one person; texts with a demanding, bossy, controlling, or demeaning tone; and texts with an overriding isolating content, trying to keep the girl from having other friends or participating in other activities. Fortunately, in most middle and high schools, the undesirable boys make up only a small percentage of the population. The rest of the boys in your daughter's world are nice, goal oriented, and definitely worthy of her attention.

Safe Strategies for Temptations

Besides cluing in your daughter to the dangers associated with alcohol, smoking, drugs, and bad boyfriends, give her some strategies to deal with the dangers. She will not always be able to contact you on the spot and ask you for advice, although these days, cell phones can be of great help. Set up a secret code system between you and your daughter. Get her to text you a certain word—the name of her pet, for example—if she needs you to come get her out of a sticky situation immediately. Being prepared while being knowledgeable to such a degree that it is almost second nature to do the right thing will help your daughter even more.

Young girls can get easily distracted, so repeatedly going over the ways your daughter can handle all kinds of tricky situations is vital. Here are those crucial strategies you want to give her verbally as well as in written form so that she can reference them:

○ If she feels uneasy about being with a group of kids, it is best to leave. Brainstorm with her a few "easy out" responses, such as she is not feeling well and needs to go home.

○ Choose a code—such as the name of her pet—that she can text to you in the event of a non-emergency situation that she wants to escape. As soon as you get the message, you will call her immediately with a good excuse to come home—now.

○ Never get in the car with someone who has been drinking, smoking pot, or popping pills, or who texts while driving. Tell her that no matter what the circumstance is, you will pick her up or arrange a ride.

○ Never accept an open drink from someone she cannot trust. Brainstorm ways to turn down a drink, such as saying she is the designated driver or finding a way to subtly throw the drink away if she feels she cannot turn it down.

Besides making sure your girl has several exit strategies imprinted on her mind when it comes to perilous situations, you want to be absolutely certain that you use the following prevention tactics yourself:

○ Network with other parents to present a united front when it comes to your children's smoking, drinking, and drug use.

○ Keep an eye on your medications and dispose of all old pills, especially painkillers.

○ Attend workshops and read up on how to address specific alcohol- and drug-related problems in your area.

○ Get to know your daughter's friends and the guidance counselor at school.

Keep in mind that the use of booze, cigarettes, and pot in teen girls often opens the door to more inappropriate conduct, even serious criminal behavior. So it is best to direct your girl's attention to more suitable pursuits. Encourage what she loves to do while keeping your eyes peeled.

Even the most enticing temptations for your daughter are opportunities for you to flex your parenting muscles. There really are no parenting concerns that you cannot deal with successfully if you make up your mind to do so, educate yourself, and reach out to other parents for advice.

Your Girl's Privacy versus Her Safety

Your daughter considers her room her castle, and she is the princess. She is right. Naturally you want her to have a haven at home where she can fling off her school clothes, plop down, and simply relax. She needs a private space where she can play her favorite music, chill out, and regroup. In many ways, her room is like her diary—you may have access only if you ask her permission.

HOME RULES

Your daughter will have no trouble telling you what she considers an invasion of her privacy. Find out what she wants you to do in regard to entering her room by asking her to fill you in. Most girls and their parents can—after discussion—come to the following understanding, or a similar one:

○ When the door is open, the parent should feel free to walk in.

○ When the door is closed, the parent should knock and wait for an answer.

○ When the parent enters, he or she should not snoop.

Since it takes time to build trust, do not break it by disregarding her rules. There are some parents who cannot wait for their daughter to leave for school so that they can rifle through her dresser drawers and closet, pry into her journal, read her e-mail, and poke through her purses. Do not join that group.

REWRITE THE RULES

As long as you feel you can count on your girl, abide by her privacy rules and respect her wishes. But if she refuses to talk to you about behavior that worries you, even after you have tried several times in a calm and respectful way to discuss her conduct, you may be forced to invade her privacy and take a closer look at her possessions. If you find something that concerns you, talk to your girl about it. Admit what you did, tell her why you did it, and assure her that together you can find a solution to the problem. Honesty is the best way to approach the situation. Assure your daughter that she can tell you anything—the fewer secrets the better. Never forget: She depends on you to be safe, to become the best she can be, and to progress rather than be waylaid by problems.

Failing Grades and Cutting School

A quick and easy way to check on how much progress your daughter is making is to measure her interest in school. Apathy toward academics is a red flag. Her role as a student is paramount. Therefore, look closely at her most recent report card. If her grades have been sliding, do not wait until the next grading period is over. Instead, put an interim report system in place.

Be sure to give your cell phone number and e-mail address to your girl's teachers and guidance counselor. Be your girl's academic coach, someone who wants to help her solve her academic dilemmas. In other words, always be a problem-solving pro in her corner, not a punisher whom she fears or avoids.

Early in the school year, identify at least one member of the faculty at your daughter's school who is accessible to parents. This does not have to be one of her teachers, although that would be nice. Build a friendship with this educator and benefit from his or her inside knowledge of the school culture and customs. Just as you work on forming a strong and unbreakable bond between you and your girl, get busy and fashion a supportive one between her and her scholastics. Your daughter should see you as an ally in her scholastic endeavors, and being involved sends that message to her.

GOOD ATTENDANCE

Besides keeping a close eye on your daughter's progress in her classes, zoom in on her attendance. Not every girl can have perfect attendance, but it is her attitude toward missing school that matters. If your daughter misses a day now and then but does her best to make up her work, you can breathe easily. If she frequently seems to seek an excuse to stay home, or you learn she is missing classes without making up the work, investigate why.

In middle and high school, skipping a class is often seen as a rite of passage. While boys usually leave the campus, girls are more likely to hide out in the bathroom. Make certain that your daughter is not lured into a ditching-class habit that rears its head every time she has a test or a term paper due. By teaching her to take a baby-step approach—doing a little schoolwork at a time—when a major exam or project looms, your daughter will be ready for the challenge and feel no need to cut school.

Internet Red Flags

The Internet can be a useful tool for a teenage girl, especially when it comes to her studies. However, when your daughter spends hours on the computer, specifically late at night, chances are that it has nothing to do with schoolwork. Remember that getting online means she is out in public—unprotected. The people she meets online and on social media sites are often not who they claim to be. So take time to go over, and update, your Internet ground rules with your daughter. Be sure to discuss the following:

O When and for what purposes she can use the Internet.

O The possibility of her being bullied, harassed, or "hit on" by others, even her classmates. She must tell you when it happens so you can help her deal with the problem, which may mean notifying the person who handles bullying at her school.

O Etiquette for posting messages and pictures online, even "privately" among friends.

OTHER RISKS

The most serious risk your daughter can face deals with the possibility of a stranger hurting her through the use of information she has posted or shared online. Warn her that interacting with people she doesn't know—via social media, e-mail, or text message—can have terrible consequences. While the number of teenage girls who are molested, kidnapped, or induced to run away from home this way is relatively small, when it does happen, the end result can be disastrous.

In reality, your daughter is more likely to be hurt by a friend or classmate than by a random stranger trolling the Internet. This can take the form of bullying, having rumors spread about her, or someone getting ahold of private information or photos and sharing them. Talk with her about both types of risks—strangers and even her friends—and brainstorm ways to keep her safe and judicious about how she interacts online.

Tell your daughter that some websites are first-class, while others are blatantly false, racist, sexist, or violent. Should she encounter one of them, she must shut down the computer immediately and tell you about it.

CHOICE PARENTS

In regard to your own use of the Internet and mobile phones, examine your lifestyle. You always want to be the best role model you can be, someone your daughter can be proud of, and someone she wants to play a robust role in her life.

Study after study shows that children with parents who are deeply involved in their lives, hold ongoing conversations with them in person and in writing, attend school events, are active in the parent-teacher organizations, and truly listen to them are less likely to drink, smoke, do drugs, or get into trouble via the Internet.

Your daughter wants you involved in every phase of her existence, but the older she gets, the more she observes. Girls, as well as boys, hate hypocrisy with a passion. There is no way you can be a closet drinker, smoker, drug-user, or visitor to questionable websites without your daughter finding out about it. You can't do wrong and still be seen as strong in her eyes.

GREATEST EXPECTATIONS

As you have the highest expectations of your daughter, she has the highest expectations of you. Do not let her down and she will not let you down. Don't worry that children never listen to their parents. Just keep in mind that raising a girl can transform you, and always for the better. How fortunate you are to have this opportunity to be the best parent and the best person you can be. Raising a girl means you are instilling and reinforcing what is best for her. At the same time, she is bringing out what is best in you.

Important Points to Consider

It is easy for parents of daughters to become fearful about the dangers of drinking, drugs, and risky behavior. Your job is to have conversations with her early on and often. The more aware and prepared you are for the risky choices your daughter will be faced with, the better able you will be to arm her with solid decision-making skills. Keep in mind the following points as you move through this conscious parenting challenge:

○ Be realistic but firm in your convictions when you talk with your daughter about experimenting with alcohol and drugs. It goes a long way toward building credibility to acknowledge that there are certain perceived benefits of experimenting, but you expect her to make positive choices. Educate her on the risks of drug and alcohol using facts, and send the message that you trust her to come to you if she has questions. Keeping an open line of communication is key.

○ Try to keep up with the latest trends in drug and alcohol use and talk with your daughter about the dangers of blindly following trends.

○ Equip your daughter with a variety of strategies to bow out of social pressures to drink or do drugs. Role-play realistic situations with her, such as a good friend encouraging her to drink at a party.

○ Make it a family policy that no matter what, she can always text or call you to pick her up from a dangerous or uncomfortable situation, such as when she is faced with getting in a car with an intoxicated driver.

○ Continue to have discussions about being safe online, including making smart choices in what she posts and how to spot potentially dangerous sites and individuals.

○ Ask your friends with children or teenagers the same age, or a professional, for parenting strategies if you feel overwhelmed. There is support available if you see your daughter taking a wrong turn.

CHAPTER 14

Health and Well-Being

Besides protecting your daughter from dangerous influences and clearing her path of obstacles, you must not overlook the routine maintenance her health and well-being require. Of course she needs her usual periodic dental and vision checkups, her annual visit to the pediatrician, and the required physicals for her sports involvement, but she also requires something more. The best way to instill good health habits in your daughter is to talk to her about them honestly. It may be difficult at times, but keeping an open line of communication and making sure your daughter knows she can come to you to talk about any issues are key to sustaining a healthy relationship throughout the years.

Her First Visit to the Gynecologist

The American Congress of Obstetricians and Gynecologists recommends that you schedule your daughter for her first visit to a gynecologist when she is between thirteen and fifteen years of age. Other experts recommend an even earlier visit. The exact age depends on the individual girl, so make sure that you keep an open dialogue with your daughter about how her body is changing. This is an exciting time for your daughter because this visit shows that she has successfully completed puberty and is now—biologically speaking—a young woman.

As a result, your girl is now ready for an appropriate physical examination, which does not have to include a pelvic exam but often does. Some girls panic when they find out they are scheduled for their first gynecological exam, which is why it's important that you mention the topic ahead of time and discuss with your girl how important all aspects of her health are. Above all, present this visit as something normal and not to be feared.

PREPARING FOR THE EXAM

Tell your daughter that getting ready for a GYN exam is like getting ready for any other medical checkup, except she should not be having her period at that time. Even better, let her choose with whom she wants to have her first one. She has the following choices:

- Her pediatrician, with whom she is familiar. Many pediatricians perform pelvic and breast exams for teenage girls.

- A gynecologist. It could be her mother's, a new one, or the one her girlfriends like.

- A nurse practitioner. This medical professional has advanced training in women's reproductive health.

- Whether or not she would prefer a female or male gynecologist. Many girls and women feel more comfortable with a woman gynecologist.

Your daughter can discuss the gynecologist options with her girl-friends, who can put her at ease and will most likely tell her that there is nothing to it. Some girls even ask their best friend along to wait in the waiting room as a support system.

REASONS FOR AN EXAM

No one likes to see a doctor for no reason, so it is best to inform your girl that her GYN exam has four main purposes:

1. A routine examination, to make sure she is developing normally

2. A preventive measure before she has sex, and to discuss birth control and sexually transmitted diseases (STDs) long before the fact, not afterward

3. A fix-it doctor visit, in case she should have problems with her periods, pain, or an infection

4. A discussion about giving your daughter an STD vaccine, unless you have already dealt with this issue

Once your daughter realizes what a great opportunity this is to ask a medical expert whatever questions have been on her mind, she may feel better about it. Advise her to write them down before the visit, so she will not forget them. If she doesn't want you in the examination room, by all means comply with her wishes. You want your girl to feel as comfortable as possible and to speak as freely as she wants to. Therefore, go over the names of her reproductive body parts with her at home before the checkup, so she will not stumble over the words or have to ask the doctor what exactly they mean. Lack of familiarity with the various terms can make her feel embarrassed, but familiarity with them will empower her.

HPV

The Centers for Disease Control and Prevention (CDC) now advise all parents to have their daughters in middle school vaccinated against the human papillomavirus (HPV). This is a common sexually transmitted disease and is—according to scientists—connected to 70 percent of all cervical cancers.

Some states now want to require that all girls entering middle school get the HPV vaccine, but some parents do not trust the immunizations. Your feelings about vaccinations should not get in the way of sound medical advice and research. Your daughter's first visit to a gynecologist is a perfect time for you and your daughter to learn about the topic of sexually transmitted diseases, specifically the HPV vaccine.

GYNECOLOGICAL TERMS

Talk to your daughter in depth about the anatomy and function of her body. If you want to, pick up an illustrated pamphlet from the doctor's office, give it to her in advance to read, and ask if she has any questions. Some daughters are very curious. They want to know all the details: the location and description of every body facet that makes them so special. Others just want to have their checkup over with and move on to other things. You know your daughter best, so you know how to handle the situation.

FAST GYN EXAM FACTS

Your daughter's first GYN exam will start with a breast exam, during which the doctor will press lightly on the various parts of your daughter's breasts and show her how to examine her own breasts. As a result, she will know which lumps are normal for her in the future. After that comes the pelvic exam, during which the doctor makes sure everything looks okay outside the vagina. Then, with the help of a speculum—a thin piece of plastic or metal—the doctor will investigate to make sure everything inside is okay as well. Sometimes the doctor will do a pap smear, which includes picking up some cells from the cervix, the opening of the uterus. Other times, this will come at a later visit. None of these procedures takes very long, so you and your daughter will have plenty of time left to schedule a special outing afterward.

AFTER THE GYN EXAM

Your daughter will most likely feel glad to have her first pelvic checkup behind her. She might tell you about some of the questions she remembered to ask, or not. But having her first female medical exam over with will make her feel more grown-up, and the next one will be a piece of cake. You, the parent, will be happy that you can check off this important event on your to-do list. Getting your girl over any awkwardness in dealing with the health of her female parts and making her smarter about every inch of her wonderful body and its upkeep is a great step. Rejoice with her. If she is quiet or lost in thought, that is all right, too. As mentioned previously, every girl reacts differently to this female checkup. Maybe up to now she had not given the intricacies of her physical being much thought. Suddenly it is dawning on her just how miraculous the workings of her body are.

In addition to changes in her body, there are also hormonal changes that can influence her mood. While some irritability and moodiness is par for the course for any adolescent, if you are starting to feel like her negative moods seem to linger longer than expected, be sure you find out why.

Girls and Depression

At any time as many as 20 percent of kids are experiencing depression—times when they seem to feel sadder or unhappier than usual. This is similar to how a cold might affect your daughter physically, except that this type of "cold" affects her emotionally.

What makes depression in girls so difficult to recognize is that it can creep in slowly. In families with more than one child, kids are often stereotyped, such as "Mark is the outgoing one, and Michelle is the quiet type." Labeling children according to their perceived personality types can be misguided and hurtful to them. The "quiet" girl may simply be quiet because she is sinking deeper and deeper into depression.

A temporary case of depression may be just part of your daughter's aches and pains as she grows up. It is to be expected in kids, who can get depressed just like adults. But since they have not developed as many coping mechanisms as their elders have, they show their depressed feelings more openly, and maybe even for longer periods. Should the sad feelings in your girl last and last, you'll want to know what to do.

THE REASONS FOR GIRLS' DEPRESSION

Approximately 8.3 percent of teens suffer from depression for at least a year at a time. Unfortunately, girls suffer from it at double the rate of boys. If you notice a serious and lasting—that is, stretching for a week or two consecutively—change in your daughter's mood, pay attention.

In your busy lifestyle, you have to keep your mind on so many things. But when you observe major changes in your girl's mood, jot down what specifically disturbs you. Does she mope all the time? Does she constantly have a somber expression? Does she seem to find absolutely no joy in her life? Chronicle what you see—if you do not write it down you might forget!—then educate yourself about the symptoms of teenage depression.

THE SYMPTOMS OF DEPRESSION

It can be difficult for you to know if your daughter is just going through a rough time emotionally or if she really is depressed. Asking her outright is usually not helpful because most girls do not know if they are depressed—they just are. So, take no chances when you notice the following in your girl:

O A big change in eating and sleeping habits

O Declining school performance and attendance

O Withdrawing from previously liked people and activities

O Persistent anxiety and unhappiness

O Constant irritability or marked silence

Then look into the situation. What can be difficult is determining if your daughter is depressed or if she is just severely sleep-deprived.

In some cases, the real problem may be another condition—bipolar disorder. This is a mental disorder that includes the opposite extremes of mania (elation and overactivity) and depression (sadness and withdrawal from activity). It used to be called manic depression before the term *bipolar disorder* was coined.

Equipping yourself with knowledge about bipolar disorder is helpful because some girls may have an episode of it during some stage of their lives. These temporary bipolar behaviors can be the result of trauma or just a fleeting occurrence. In girls, the basic signs of bipolar disorder can resemble what is fairly normal in teen behavior. But it is the persistence and duration of these signs you want to watch out for, not the one-time occurrence of them.

Parents of girls with bipolar disorder frequently report that their daughters' periods are problematic. Either the girls have long absences of menstruation or much longer cycles, or they experience heavy bleeding and extreme cramping. Therefore, visit the gynecologist to discuss this particular problem any time your girl's periods are very irregular or accompanied by a lot of pain.

THE SIGNS OF BIPOLAR DISORDER

If you are worried your daughter is suffering from bipolar disorder, take on the role of record keeper. Make a note if you observe the following in your girl:

O Severe difficulty in sleeping

O Fast, nonstop talking, racing thoughts, and seemingly unlimited energy

O Frequent mood changes—up and down, down and up

○ Risky behavior

There can be still more characteristics depending on the individual girl. None of these behaviors alone, or occurring only for a short time, is extremely worrisome, but in combination and long-term, they should concern you.

PARENTAL WISDOM

Remember those times when your little girl used to come to you crying because she stumbled and hurt herself, or the wheel of her tricycle fell off, or her favorite teddy bear lost a leg? Remember how you told her then that you would make it all better? You picked her up, kissed her, put a bandage on her knee, fixed the tricycle, and sewed on the stuffed-animal limb. You proved to her that you were powerful in making her feel better.

Now do the same thing. Really make it all better. That starts with putting your arm around your daughter's shoulder and telling her that you will fix this, too—whatever her problem may be. Whether it is depression, bipolar disorder, or any of the serious health concerns detailed in the following pages, the very first thing you always want to do is reassure your daughter that you will find the answer to her issues no matter what. She is not alone and can always count on you. You will indeed do everything you can to make things better for her and will not rest until the issues are resolved.

Sit down with her and repeat these statements, and then tell her that in some cases the best any parent can do is reach beyond her expertise and enlist the help of experts in the medical field. You do not want to try several halfhearted approaches on your own only to waste time before finally finding one that works. No, in serious matters like her emotional and physical health and well-being, you are starting at once and are going straight to the top.

TOP PARENT PLAN

In cases of serious health matters—mental or otherwise—that concern your daughter, you have to spring into action immediately. You want to waste no time before taking these steps:

1. Make an appointment with a medical or mental health professional as soon as possible and get your girl some help.

2. Be more supportive of her than ever, listen to her, and don't criticize.

3. Become the most informed parent you can be via the library, local support groups, and the Internet.

Thus, you are using the full power of your love and care for your daughter in combination with all the knowledge of the health experts. Then, working together, fiercely attack the problem. Using all your resources and theirs, keep at it until you make some headway. After all, this is your chance to show what a truly remarkable and conscious parent you are.

Suicide Warning Signs

Today's movies, music, video games, and other media can lead many young girls to believe that suicide is a glorious experience. Added to that are easy access to weapons, pills in the medicine cabinet at home, and the glamorization of a drug overdose. Some girls go so far as to mention their suicidal leanings to their friends but swear them to secrecy. Please warn your daughter about that possibility and tell her that the consequences of keeping quiet could be tragic. Should her friend commit suicide, your daughter would feel a horrible burden of guilt for the rest of her life. Therefore, tell her to let you know immediately when a girl in her circle mentions suicide, especially when she mentions it more than once, even just in a joking manner.

A phrase such as "I'll kill myself if I don't get asked to the prom" may just be part of a teen girl's everyday verbal chitchat. But when this statement is repeated over and over with a somber expression and with tears cascading down her face, the girl's friends need to listen. Maybe there is more to it. Teach your daughter to do the following:

O Keep an eye out for any friend who seems to be sad for an unusually long time.

○ Be alert for friends posting hopeless, helpless, or depressive thoughts online.

○ Encourage her friend to look for help and go with her to the guidance counselor.

○ Discuss what worries her about her friend with you or another trusted adult.

Besides listening to your daughter and her friends' conversations for any hints of a possible suicide, a parent needs to be familiar with the associated risk factors.

SUICIDE RISK FACTORS

Once you know the risk factors for suicide in girls, you can be especially watchful in regard to not only your daughter but also the girls in her group. Plus, you can pass on this information to other parents and make them aware as well. Who knows, you might even save a young life.

Here are the risk factors for teenage suicide:

○ Previous suicide attempts or having a close family member who committed suicide

○ Recent tragic losses, such as the death of a loved one, parents' divorce, or a breakup with a boyfriend

○ Social aloneness—no friends or activities to engage in

○ Drug or alcohol abuse—drugs and alcohol can decrease impulse control, making impulsive suicide more apt to occur

○ Loaded weapons in the home

○ The presence of depression, an eating disorder, or another medical condition

However, the good news is that most suicidal girls send up plenty of red flags about their intentions. Of course they do; they want someone to notice. So in addition to paying attention to any suicidal talk between your daughter and her friends, watch out for other crucial signs.

> Some researchers believe there are two groups of suicidal teens. One is the long-term chronically or severely depressed group. The suicide attempts by this group are carefully planned. The other group may not be as severely depressed and acts more impulsively and on the spur of the moment, using whatever method is handy at the time.

There are other signs of impending suicide in a girl. Some can be quite noticeable and should be eye opening. For example, teenage girls usually "love" their favorite clothes, shoes, purses, CDs, and movies. When they suddenly start giving them all away, investigate why. Also watch out for any girl preoccupied with death and dying, taking excessive risks, being extremely depressed, or acting very differently from the way she used to.

BEST HEALTH NEWS

The excellent good news is that the mental health field has made enormous strides in this area. Depressed girls can now be treated early, before they go too far. You and your daughter have all kinds of treatment options available these days, should she need them. There is talk therapy, a vast array of new antidepressant medicines, and—most often recommended— a combination of both. Know that you have available to you many top doctors, psychiatrists, and psychologists. All you have to do is call upon their expertise right away. You really must not hesitate to do so should your girl experience any of the following disorders, which are impossible to overcome without professional help.

Anorexia, Bulimia, and Other Eating Disorders

Eating disorders, including anorexia nervosa, bulimia, and binge eating, can be among the most difficult problems your daughter could develop. Because these disorders deal with what girls should have a good relationship with—daily nourishment—and can appear in so many different and scary forms, parents are often in denial. By the time a parent wakes up, the problems a girl has can be deeply ingrained and even harder to eradicate.

The two most common eating disorders are anorexia, which involves extremely restricted eating, and bulimia, which involves overeating and purging (either through use of laxatives or by inducing vomiting). According to the Dove Campaign for Real Beauty global report, up to 13 percent of girls age 15–17 acknowledge having an eating disorder. The National Institute of Mental Health estimates that eating disorders affect more than 5 million Americans each year. Approximately 5 percent of adolescent and adult woman have anorexia or bulimia, which means 5 out of every 100 girls suffer from a clinical eating disorder.

NO BLAME GAME

If you suspect that your girl has an eating disorder, don't waste time blaming yourself for not noticing sooner. Most girls with eating disorders cloak themselves in secrecy—at least at the beginning. Additionally, some girls who are perfectly healthy otherwise can suddenly develop one of these disorders and leave their families dumbfounded. All these diseases are thought to occur because of a teenage girl's problem with her body image. But the answers are not as clear-cut as they may seem. Boys can also have eating disorders, and older adults often admit they have had them for years.

EATING DISORDER PREVENTION

Preventing eating disorders sounds easy but is hard. By the time your daughter is an adolescent, you do not have much control over her body, exercise, or eating. Of course you should avoid criticizing her about her appearance, her weight, or what she eats, and not compare her to other girls. It is better to encourage her to exercise appropriately and serve her healthful foods. But sometimes these actions are not enough. There may also be a strong hereditary component that you can do nothing about. What you can do is keep on the lookout for these warning signs:

○ Losing weight at an alarming rate

○ Losing and gaining weight like a yo-yo

○ Talking a lot about being fat

○ Barely eating anything or eating secretly

○ Exercising to excess

○ Spending much time in the bathroom after meals, or always running to the restroom during dinner

This is only a partial list. Should you have any concerns about your daughter's weight—either being too little or too much—talk to her doctor at once. When dealing with eating disorders, every hour counts, so do not wait until the following occurs:

○ Your girl eats only crumbs, develops a vomiting habit, chews laxatives like candy, and spins out of control with overactivity.

○ Your girl is tired and weak all the time, stops having periods, develops baby hair all over her body and thinning hair on her head.

○ Your girl ends up in the emergency room with heart problems, looking like nothing but skin and bones, and just barely clinging to life.

You are too strong, too smart, and too alert a parent to let this happen. Remind yourself that you will put an end to whatever derailment in relationship to eating your daughter has developed, and you will be watchful in other areas of her growth as well. You may feel overwhelmed and out of control when you see your daughter in pain, but one of the best ways to help her is to show love, support, and empathy.

Self-Mutilation and Intervention

Self-mutilation is the general term for a girl hurting herself without intent to commit suicide. The most common behavior is cutting herself with a razor, but it can also include biting herself, bruising herself, burning herself, or amputating parts of her body.

Many researchers think self-mutilation is the result of a girl feeling shame or her wish to relieve an unbearable tension within her. It can also be an expression of anger at someone else that is instead directed toward the girl herself. What makes it worse is that "cutters" always try to hide their scars from the public. So you have to wonder what is going on if your daughter walks around covered from head to toe all year—even in mid-July.

CAUSES

When you find your daughter in pain, you hurt. The more she suffers, the more you do. So end the suffering for both of you—now. Seek immediate professional help when you learn of your daughter hurting herself. Many girls who self-mutilate in whatever form are in an agony worse than you can imagine. Sometimes this behavior is a sign that a girl feels dead inside and the sensation of pain gives her a momentary feeling that she is alive.

Many girls who harm themselves have experienced something truly awful, such as:

○ An overwhelming trauma

○ Sexual abuse as a child or tween

○ Severe physical abuse

○ Emotional neglect, starvation, or imprisonment

There is also a growing group of girls who are not in significant pain but are experimenting with cutting themselves because they have seen or heard of a peer doing so. In the same way a teen may experiment with smoking or drinking, she may be experimenting with cutting as a "coping mechanism," because her peers are doing it. Your job is to find out if she is experimenting or is a serious cutter—either way, seek professional guidance right away.

INTERVENTION
Should you sense or see any signs of self-mutilation in your daughter or her friends, take charge immediately. Write down or take a photo of what you see, and take your observations to a professional. Probe into the past. Find out if anything has happened to your daughter and when. You may not be able to tease out if there has been a traumatic event on your own, so ally with a mental health professional to do a trauma screening. Even more important, see to it that your daughter knows you are intervening so she can start healing—from this moment on. She may try to downplay the significance of her behavior, but you want to send the message that even if the risk is small, you love her so much that you want to make sure all is well and set her up with ongoing support if she needs it.

Runaway Signals

Sometimes a girl has been hurt so badly that she sees no other solution than to run away. Her natural instinct is to escape from something she feels she cannot go through again. Or maybe she has done something her parents told her not to do and she feels she will never be forgiven. So she packs a few things into her bookbag and starts hitchhiking—not knowing that she could end up in serious danger. Most runaway girls give signs that they are thinking about leaving home. These signs can include the following:

○ Your girl acts completely unsociable.

- Your girl hangs out with kids who drink, use drugs, or have run away before.

- Your girl steals money from you, which she hoards.

- Your girl starts staying out all night, with no explanation given.

If your daughter seriously withdraws from the family, makes secret plans, or talks about running away, call in the cavalry—all those experts and professionals ready and waiting to help: the guidance counselors, school psychologists, social workers, psychiatrists, and medical doctors. There are a huge number of specialists poised to help you. To think you have to solve your problem by yourself is a huge mistake. When you have a problem with your roof, you call in someone to fix it right away. When you have a problem with the core of your life, your darling daughter, set everything aside and go to battle for her. Trust that the caring cavalry will fight side by side with you until victory is achieved.

Do you remember how your daughter was as a little girl? How she always came to you back then? Now come to her and help heal her. Forget about your heavy heart. Forget feeling like you have let her down. Now you have another chance. As the old saying goes, a daughter may outgrow your lap, but she will never outgrow your heart. As soon as you help your daughter onto the road to recovery, your heartache will begin to ease.

Important Points to Consider

Your daughter's health and well-being are of paramount importance. Having a healthy body and making healthy choices start with preventive care and awareness of warning signs for unhealthy behavior. Keep in mind the following points:

- Schedule your daughter for her first gynecologist appointment and give her a heads-up about what to expect. Do not be offended if she does not want you in the room with her. It is better for her to have a place where she can get her questions answered than to sit in silence with you in the room.

○ Even before your daughter is sexually active, partner with her gynecologist in educating her on prevention of unwanted pregnancy and sexually transmitted diseases.

○ Educate yourself on other risks to your daughter's health, including signs of depression and anxiety. Intervene early when warning signs are present and seek help if you are not sure how to help her with her challenges.

○ More extreme acting-out behaviors such as self-harm and running away are causes for immediate intervention with a professional at your side. Do not be ashamed to ask for help right away. This is the first step toward keeping her safe and beginning the healing process.

CHAPTER 15

Your Daughter and Sexuality

Nothing can scare parents more than their daughter's sexuality. This term encompasses her behavior, impulses, and feelings connected to her as a sexual being. Mention *sexuality* in connection with their girl, and many parents immediately worry about STDs, pregnancy, and her life being ruined forever. But not you. You are the type of thoughtful, conscious parent who realizes that this aspect of your daughter is a chance for you to inform her, guide her, and make sure she can fully rejoice in her sexuality, but only when the time is right.

Teaching Your Daughter about Sex

If you don't teach your daughter about her body, sex, and sexuality, her friends will be more than happy to do so, and they are far less likely than you to have the correct information. Many parents think there is only one major talk about sexuality and sex they should have with their daughter. In actuality, there are three crucial discussions you should have with your girl:

1. What's happening with her body?

2. What's happening with boys' bodies?

3. What is intercourse and when is it appropriate?

The reason most parents feel awkward about even one of the three talks—let alone all of them—is that their parents did not talk with them about sex. These days, however, sex is exerting its influence in every aspect of our lives, and especially the lives of young people. Your daughter will be curious about her body and how it functions early on.

Some parents also feel embarrassed when discussing sex with their daughter because they cannot acknowledge that their baby has grown into a sexual being. Or perhaps they made mistakes when they were young, still regret them, and want to make sure their girl does not do likewise. So their conversation on sex may not have the smoothest delivery. But remember, your own attitude about sex is important. Educate yourself as much as possible so you are informed and not easily shocked. Your daughter should feel that you are relaxed and approachable and willing to talk to her about sex. If you show your daughter that you are comfortable with the topic, she will be more likely to feel at ease as well.

THE TALK

You certainly want to collect your thoughts and feel comfortable with the subject matter before you launch into your sex talk with your daughter. To gain a sense of comfort, educate yourself about common changes in puberty for both males and females. Remember, if you are uncomfortable your child will sense it and will adopt that uneasiness. There are three common approaches to speaking to your daughter about sex, and not all of them are good choices:

1. Handing your daughter a book and otherwise avoiding the topic completely.

2. Using scare tactics and telling your daughter she will make a big mistake if she becomes sexually active.

3. Discussing openly and honestly with your daughter the pros and cons of sexual activity at this stage of her life.

You want to use the third approach. If you feel uncomfortable with it, go with the first approach—the book—as a way to segue into the third approach, which is to follow up with a long talk during which you point out what a healthy relationship with a boy entails, what your family's values are, and how your girl should handle sexual matters. You can also look at/read a book *with* your daughter, which can sometimes ease discomfort or awkwardness and give you a place to focus your attention while still being present to answer additional questions. Using scare tactics shows a lack of communication and trust that will make her uncomfortable speaking with you about sex and may force her to explore her sexuality in secret.

Unless prescribed for medical reasons, you should not just put your daughter on birth control when she reaches a certain age. Randomly putting your daughter on birth control pills shows her that you do not trust her to be an intelligent, independent-thinking girl who has good values and can make smart choices. Instead, sit down and talk with her, and do that often.

Do not have just one sex talk with your child and then never say another word about it. Sexuality is in the forefront of the lives of teenagers, so it should become one of the things you discuss often with your daughter. Keep the lines of communication open. Tell her stories about how you found out about sex when you were young, and show your girl that today's openness in sex talks is so much better than the silence and ignorance of the past. During the "talk," you may want to lay some ground rules.

WHEN THE TIME IS RIGHT

Don't feel as though you have to give your daughter all the information on every possible situation all at once. Give her age-appropriate information throughout her life.

- **Birth to two years old:** Use the correct names for parts of the body so she can learn them.

- **Three to four years old:** Answer truthfully your child's questions about the differences between boys' and girls' bodies. Discuss what it means to be female or male. Remember, children at this age can retain only about one main fact per conversation.

- **Five to eight years old:** Children this age are curious about how babies are born and what pregnant women go through. Answer their questions honestly. They may also have questions on breast development, menstruation, and growth of body hair. Reassure your daughter that the changes in her body are normal and may happen at different times for different girls.

- **Nine to twelve years old:** At this stage you might want to talk to your daughter about intercourse and its consequences. Also talk about pregnancy and disease prevention. Encourage your daughter to come to you with any questions regarding her body or things she may hear other kids saying. Support her talking to you about things she hears from her friends. Remember to be open and willing to talk about any concerns, no matter what they may be.

- **Thirteen to eighteen years old:** Continue to communicate with your daughter and give clear messages about your concerns and values. Encourage your daughter to think independently and with self-confidence about sex because as she grows older she will be making these sexual decisions on her own.

While you may be concerned about answering your young girl's sexual questions honestly, be aware that being knowledgeable can help protect her from molestation and coercion from older teens and adults. Knowing that she can discuss sexual matters with you at any time will make her less likely to keep any inappropriate talking or touching a secret.

Be sure to inform your daughter that many sexual myths exist and it's important to have the facts. For example, she *can* get pregnant the first time she has sex, she *can* get pregnant when she has her period, she *can* get an infection from oral sex, and boys *can* relieve themselves of sexual tension without her help.

SEX INFORMATION

You have always encouraged your girl to unburden herself with her friends and listen to them, too. When it comes to sex, however, your daughter should continue to talk to her friends about what she has on her mind, but she should be cautious about what her friends say. Tell your girl that in sexual matters:

1. Her girlfriends may have little, if any, correct information.

2. Her boyfriends may be worse off; they may know even fewer actual facts.

3. Society and advertising can confuse her with their sexual messages.

4. You, her parents, are a reliable source.

Encourage your daughter to share with you any concerns or questions she may have about what she has heard her peers discussing. Be ready for the majority of information your daughter has been told to be incorrect and be comfortable enough to explain to your daughter the true facts. Promise to give her the latest and best knowledge there is, and then—and only then—should she even think about considering having sex.

Also teach your daughter a few great comebacks that she can use when being pressured into having sex. When a boy says, "Why not? Everybody's doing it," she can reply, "I've got news for you. I'm not everybody." Or when her girlfriends prod her with, "If you love him, you have to do it with him," she can say, "If he loves me, he can wait."

No matter how great your relationship is with your girl, she may still feel uncomfortable talking about sex with you. If she shuts down or refuses to talk on this topic, don't be offended or throw up your hands and say, "Well, I tried!" Tell her you are always there for her if she wants to talk and also suggest she reach out to a trusted adult, such as a favorite aunt, her doctor, or a family friend whom you know will dispense sound information and advice.

NO MORE RUSH

Nowadays most girls prepare themselves for college, get degrees, and start their careers long before they begin to think about settling down. After a few years, they might get married, but not in haste. More and more women are taking time to explore their career possibilities and who they are as individuals before entering a lifelong relationship.

Girls today have at least ten glorious years, which girls of the past did not have, to make a mark in their chosen professions. These ten independent years are wonderful times for girls to forge a path with meaningful work, to travel and see the world, and to meet a wide array of possible life partners. Why should modern girls throw away these ten years getting embroiled in physical relationships with boys who still have a long way to go before they are grown up?

NO RANDOM ROMANCE

Allow your daughter to think about what you have told her and ask her to map out a long-range plan for herself. Just as she has a scholastic plan, she should have a sexual plan. She should decide when it will be appropriate for her to become intimate (hopefully not for at least a few years) and what she is looking for in a partner (hopefully someone she cares about who also cares for her). Clue her in that while many teenagers seem to be having sex, the reality is that many are also waiting until the time is right. Assure her that she can enjoy her sexuality without having sex, and that if she chooses to have sex, it is not always a "bad thing" if she is smart about protecting herself—both her feelings and her body.

Girls who feel they have strong, supportive parents with whom they can have many conversations about sex and values appear to be more resistant to the sexual messages and pressures of our culture. Parents should acknowledge that their daughter's decision is not simple. They should not say all sex is bad but discuss the topic in detail, including conversations about how emotional connection can enhance sexual experiences, the protective measures she and her partner will need to discuss before having sex, what consent is, how to consent or not, and avoiding risky sexual situations. In the end, parental expectations and having frank discussions about sex can have a great effect on girls.

There are a number of books dedicated solely to this topic of girls and sexuality that parents can explore. A Mighty Girl has a resource list for parents at www.amightygirl.org.

Promiscuity

Not enough parents talk to their daughters about promiscuity, a pattern of behavior that is characterized by casual sex with many partners. Instead, they just hope that their daughter is not promiscuous. Hope alone does not suffice in this case.

Talk to her about the dangers of promiscuity, which include the following:

○ Ending up with emotional baggage, which can result from disappointing one's parents, gaining a reputation that has social consequences at school, and the fear of pregnancy and sexually transmitted diseases.

○ Having bad sexual experiences, the chances of which increase with the number of partners a girl has.

○ Not being able to develop a relationship after casual sex. Boys sometimes do not feel an emotional attachment to a girl after sex the way girls do.

Count on this: Your daughter will weigh your words carefully. She knows you cannot follow her around wherever she goes and prevent her from deviating from her plan to delay having sex until after high school, until she has found her true love, or until she is married. But when you make talking about sex comfortable long before she gets close to thinking about having sex, she will remember what you said. She will make the right choices for her. But even before she has her first boyfriend, she really should think about all the issues involved.

"Hooking Up" versus a Relationship

Let your daughter know that there are distinct differences between entering into a meaningful relationship and having a casual "hookup." When a girl hooks up with a boy who is a friend, the arrangement is sometimes referred to as "friends with benefits." The hookup, a now-common phenomenon, is an impulse action that does not lead to a serious loving relationship and can sometimes be a sign of poor self-esteem and lack of confidence. It also could negatively affect her reputation. A relationship, however, is a meaningful venture in which both parties feel valued and cared for.

HOOKING UP

These days hooking up (a quick sexual involvement that may only last one night and occurs between strangers or mere acquaintances) gets much attention on college campuses. Since whatever scenes play out at the universities can filter down to high schools, your daughter may already have seen some examples of kids in her grade hooking up. They have definitely been talking about it. So do not be surprised when your girl mentions the phenomenon. Tell her that this is nothing new. It used to be called a one-night stand, and it is an extremely unwise practice. Not only does a girl who hooks up not know anything about her partner—or his sexual history—but she may also feel depersonalized and demeaned if he blows her off and never talks to her again.

According to a report by Planned Parenthood, about 30 percent of all teenage girls—three in every ten—become pregnant before age twenty.

There is little research on the psychological effects of casual sexual encounters, or hooking up, among teenage girls. The research that has been done on college students and young adults suggests that motivations for hooking up, perceptions of hookup culture, feelings after hooking up, and differences between men and women are conflicting. You will want to discuss with your daughter that even though hookups are seen as more socially acceptable these days, there may be unanticipated consequences to casual sexual encounters, both physically and emotionally.

Teach Your Daughter to Say No

To grow up as well as possible and to explore all her potential as a teenager, your daughter needs to be empowered to be strong and to soldier on. If you teach her how to say no to sex—loudly and clearly—she will be especially powerful. You want to equip her with the power to consent to sex or not, as well as to avoid situations where she feels uncomfortable saying no or is compromised in her decision-making. She is too young to put her intellectual growth on hold. However, premature intimate entanglements where the lines of consent are blurred can do just that. So give your girl all the tools you can to help her stave off society's and the teenage world's pressures in regard to sex. Teach her that she is in charge of her body and her choice to have sex when she is ready.

GIRL COURAGE

As with all parenting situations, give addressing the sexual part of your daughter's development your best shot. Tell her it is in her best interest to concentrate on her number-one job in her teen years: being a great student and participating in many extracurricular activities. Sex can always come later. Once she finishes high school successfully, she can have more freedom. For now, she should have as much fun as possible as a teenager and not burden herself with worries about birth control, sexually transmitted diseases, and emotional consequences of being pressured to have sex before she is ready.

Your Daughter Is Attracted to Other Girls

When you observe your daughter having crushes on other girls, realize this can be a normal stage of her sexual development. Beginning in elementary school girls will often idolize a pretty young female teacher or admire an older girl from afar. Later they may develop an extremely close relationship with one girlfriend and focus primarily on her. At age twelve or thirteen, some girls even start role-playing games with a group of curious girls where one is chosen to play the part of the boy, and the other girls practice their kissing skills on "him." They may take turns being the pretend-male, or they may ask for volunteers.

Many girls start to experiment with same-sex relationships and bisexuality as they grow up. This is a normal passing phase for them. Only time will indicate your daughter's true sexuality. No matter what you may think, you cannot choose it for her.

Growing up, your daughter can take a circuitous path. So be ready for almost anything and enjoy watching your girl make the journey from her early to her late teens. Let her be herself as her identity unfolds and accept whatever sexual orientation it turns out she develops. No matter how strong the beliefs of some groups, research tells us that girls do not choose to be homosexual or heterosexual. What if your girl comes to you and tells you she thinks she belongs to that group?

BRAVE GIRL

If your daughter reveals to you that she is gay (also known as "coming out"), give her a big hug and tell her you are proud of her. It takes courage for a girl to be honest with her parents about her sexual preference while still in high school. But also hug yourself—in spirit. You are to be commended for having done such a good job as a parent that your daughter can come to you. Tell her you are so very, very proud of her—just the way she is.

While our culture has come a long way toward being more accepting of what were once regarded as alternative lifestyles, your daughter may still encounter some challenges related to her sexuality. You may also have some strong feelings about her sexuality, due to you or your spouse's personal beliefs about homosexuality as well as awareness of the types of struggles she may face in life. As a conscious parent, though, you want to walk with your daughter, arm-in-arm, being an empathic listener and her strongest ally. She needs your support more than ever, and this gives you even more chances to expand your parenting skills and to surpass what you have done so far.

Important Points to Consider

In regard to sex, you expect your daughter to handle herself with the same intelligence, thoughtfulness, and dignity she exhibits in all other aspects of her life. Always hold her to the highest standards. But should she make a slip, let her know that she can always come to you and tell you the truth—she must never forget that. Although you may not condone whatever she did, you will carry her emotionally through her troubled moments. Keep in mind the following as you guide her during this important phase of her development:

○ The more comfortable you are with having discussions about sexuality and sex with your daughter, the more open the lines of communication will be. This could feel awkward or uncomfortable at first, especially if your parents never talked to you about sex. You can acknowledge this with your daughter and then sally forth—it is better to awkwardly open the lines of communication than to leave lessons about sex to her peers or mainstream culture.

○ Lessons about sex and body consent start way before your daughter is sexually active. At each stage in her life, you can talk with her about changes in her body, sexual feelings, and how her body is hers and hers alone to make decisions about.

○ Be authentic with your daughter about sexuality. Give her the facts about teen pregnancy and sexually transmitted diseases as well as how to decide when she is ready for sex.

○ Be aware of the "hookup culture" that may abound in your daughter's social circle. Just because it's "normal" among peers doesn't mean it's necessarily right for your daughter and her emotional state. Talk with her about her values, warn her of the potential hazards of casual sex, and advise her not to engage in behavior that she later will regret.

○ No matter how your daughter expresses her sexuality, know that you are still a strong player in helping her through this important time. Keep the lines of communication open, or offer a trusted resource for her if she is not comfortable talking with you.

CHAPTER 16

From Girl to Woman

There will come a day when all the tough and thoughtful lessons you have taught your daughter come together to produce a wonderful human being—your girl all grown up. As she grew from infancy to her tween and teen stages, you were there for her, supporting her and loving her. Now she is becoming an adult capable of making her own decisions and mapping her own journey through life. This is the time you can begin to ease up, let go, and admire the young woman you have raised.

Your Daughter As a Young Woman

As a young woman, your daughter is self-reliant, confident, and independent thinking. She is ready to venture into the world and make good choices. You have loved her from the moment she was born, all through her baby years, her elementary school experiences, on and on, and she has now advanced to her grown-up stage.

During all these years you taught her everything you know, and with this knowledge she can now stand on her own two feet. She may make some mistakes, but without messing up and figuring out what went wrong, your daughter would not have a chance to progress. Remember that. If she were "perfect" in every way, she would be a marble statue, not the warmhearted, strong, and determined example of the best of young womanhood.

Be sure to tell your daughter that success for a woman has many definitions. It may mean great accomplishments, such as earning a graduate degree, publishing articles in international journals, and speaking to thousands. Or it may be growing a vegetable garden and taking the tomatoes to the local soup kitchen. Or perhaps it will be reading to a sick child in a hospital room. The trick is learning who you are as a woman and being thrilled about it.

Competing in the World

What you are doing is miraculous. You have been raising a girl who wants to succeed and proves it every day. She is willing to do her best to achieve and does not shirk competition, and the news could not be better in this regard. This is the century of the smart, independent-thinking, productive girl.

GOING TO COLLEGE

One example to prove that this century is the best era ever for girls is the scene on today's American college campuses. For the first time in American history the tide has turned. Female students now outnumber male students by four to three. In fact, women receive 57 percent of the bachelor's degrees these days, while men get only 43 percent.

This development will make college a very welcoming and inviting place for your daughter. Many of her classes will be female oriented. Many of the organizations at the university she attends will be run by girls or even be dominated by them. Even her chances of getting into a field she likes may increase because more women-oriented courses of study will be added. In short, the era of the "big man on campus" has just turned into the era of the "wonderful woman on campus."

Your daughter is fortunate to be part of the new girls-in-power movement that shows itself more and more in high school and truly emerges in college. While the deans of admissions have to worry about how to get more boys to apply, your daughter has nothing but advantages awaiting her once she gets there. Of course, more girls going to college than ever before may mean the competition is getting stiffer. But so what? Your daughter will welcome this challenge when she is old enough for it. She will be well prepared because you have gotten her primed in advance.

GIRLS' TOP TACTICS

You and your daughter may have discussed her going to college someday. If she seems interested in college, or even if she is not, start talking now, no matter what grade she is in, and encourage her studies. Her academic training, bolstered by your interest and guidance at home, will help her get there. Of course, she has to have a high grade point average (GPA) and do well on the required admission tests.

While girls usually make higher grades in high school than boys, boys usually score higher on their SATs. One reason for that is that girls can get too concerned about finding the perfect test answer while boys tend to guess more accurately and use the test time period more wisely.

Long before your girl needs to take the SAT or the ACT, or both, allow her to look at those tests, or at least a section of them. Take away the fear of the unknown by keeping a practice book lying around on the kitchen table. Mark up the book, dog-ear the pages, and rip out a word list or two. Every so often pick out a question at random and together with your daughter, answer it—or try to. Demystify the college application process by telling your girl that all her good work inside and outside the classroom will be considered and not only her GPA.

Try your best to get your daughter over the notion that she cannot make a mistake when she applies. Her essay should not sound as though it was written by a brilliant robot but by a real girl. One essay option a college recently offered to prospective students was, "Tell us about something you did that was just plain fun." So, make sure your girl's life is filled with a good combination of studying and enjoyable activities. Also, get on the Internet and have admissions officers from numerous schools send you their glossy brochures and their facts on financial aid packages, and let them compete for your tuition cash. It is fun to look at the inviting pictures with your girl and highlight the strengths the various schools have to offer and at what price—in other words, to comparison-shop.

COMPETING IN BUSINESS

As a parent, all you need to do is tell your daughter to do her personal best when it comes to competing in the job market. That personal best varies from daughter to daughter, but your girl knows what it means for her, and that is all that matters. She should already know how to compete in academics and athletics, and this skill can translate to applying for college and scholarships and performing well in job interviews, in the workplace, and in whatever other opportunities may crop up. To ensure that your daughter can handle the competition, explain the following:

O She should know that this world is made up of many competitive environments.

O She should be able to accept whatever pressures these competitive environments place on her, find a career mentor, and aim straight for the top.

O She should learn to depressurize whatever competitive environment she ends up in and learn how to cope with and alleviate stress.

○ Most of all, she should go with her own plans and opt out of any competitive environment any time she chooses.

That is another huge advantage of being a girl these days. She can leap at whatever competitive endeavors she likes and log off any time she has had enough. Your daughter can change her plans, a little or a lot, and nobody can stop her. She is empowered to be herself.

As she grows, your daughter may change a lot. Your daughter must always feel free to fight her battles and put her competitive drive into high gear—or to make peace, slow down, and choose her own winding path. As a girl today, she has more choices than any previous generation, male or female.

DEALING WITH SETBACKS

If your daughter's first college or career plan does not pan out, she should not feel a sense of failure. Obviously, she is meant for something else, something better, and something far greater. Many girls have so many talents that it is a joy for the parents to watch them explore one after the other. Just as food tastes better with spices added in, your daughter's life will perk up even more when she tries her hand at one job and then another, or when she switches from one major to another in college.

Tell your girl about the many times you have changed your mind about something. It meant your mind was alive and working. Tell her about the incredible journey she is making from girl to woman. There may be a few side trips and some meandering along the way. She should enjoy the infinite variety of her possibilities. Girls who never have a setback will be ill equipped in our quickly changing world that each day adds more options to everyone's menu. The ultimate test of any activity or endeavor for your daughter is to ask herself if it fits her. If it does, that's great. If it does not, that's even better. Let the next stage of her life's sojourn begin with all its new chances.

Mentoring Your Daughter-Friend

To be a mentor means to be an experienced advisor and supporter, and you are that. As a conscious parent with now close to twenty years of experience, there is no one more qualified than you to give advice to your daughter, watch over her, and foster her progress. In business, mentoring connects the most successful employee with a new or inexperienced colleague. In politics, acting, and athletics, mentoring is also very much en vogue. In fact, many of the most successful people in the world have gained enormously from a mentor.

Think about what it means to truly be your daughter's mentor. You will make the transition from your child's manager to her facilitator and ultimately her confidant and mentor. Take your mentor role as seriously as you can and share with your daughter all your secrets for successful living.

INTERNET AND TEXT MENTORING

You have a great advantage in mentoring your daughter: the latest technology. You do not have to write out lengthy letters, hustle them to the post office, hope she checks her mailbox once in a while, and then wait for her to reply, if she can even find the time with all the new activities and demands that fill her life away from home. You have a better way of staying in touch with your daughter by simply:

○ Texting her daily with a word of encouragement, e-mailing her your best advice, or leaving your thoughts on a topic she brought up on her voicemail.

○ Forwarding her book reviews, articles, and blogs of interest.

○ If you live close by, scheduling regular visits with her, or meeting halfway between your locations every month for brunch.

○ If you are far away, planning visits and/or getaway vacations with her.

○ Skyping/Facetiming with her every weekend or getting in touch with her via social media.

○ Texting her pictures and asking her to send you some as well.

The best thing about any new-technology mentoring of your daughter is that you can present her with new ways of thinking, a path to new opportunities, and tons of fresh resources—at a distance. So no hurt feelings while she decides whether to take your counsel or not. You made the offer. You put your well-meaning thoughts out there. That is all you can do. She has to choose for herself what fits with her life's format and future. The next day you can again send more advice or lots of compliments her way. In fact, by using all the plus points of cyberspace, you can reduce the space separating you and your daughter to nothing more than the split second it takes to click the mouse or hit send on your phone. A terrific text—short and sweet—is the most immediate communication there is so far.

Empty Nest Equals Wider Circle

Some parents begin lamenting the "empty nest syndrome" they fear they will experience when their daughter leaves, starting with the time she enters high school. All parents have their own modus operandi, so to speak. Many, however, seem to enjoy the past more than the moment of parental achievement. They also suffer and wallow in anticipation of a daughterless home, rather than realize that all they need to do is widen their home front. They should just incorporate the college campus where their daughter is or the new town she has chosen to work in into their lives. Instead of an empty nest, parents whose girl has gone off into the world simply have a bigger nest.

NO REGRETS

It is human nature to want what you cannot have either by looking ahead into the future or by wishing you had another chance to do over the past. Parents who fear that they did not give their best efforts in raising their daughter tend to regret their lost opportunities and bemoan the fact that she flew the coop too soon. While the parenting chances that moms and dads let slip away are indeed gone, it is never too late to start over. Even disengaged fathers and mothers can make a new start any time.

Parenting is not a one-time act but a continuum during which parents can decide to re-engage in their child rearing and give their best efforts to their daughter—from now on. What can prevent some parents from doing this is that they spend too much time feeling sorry for themselves once their daughter leaves. They find themselves crying for no reason, snapping at people, being melancholy, or feeling that life is passing them by.

NEW SEASON

There is nothing wrong with being wistful and thoughtful, even wishful, as a parent. Now you are alone at home and have no extra laundry to do or big messes to clean up. So enjoy having fewer chores, welcome this new wonderful season, and live it up. Take time now to do the following:

- Express some of those long-neglected talents you have. Take a class or join a new group.

- Indulge in the dreams and desires you have tabled for so long. Work on yourself or take up new hobbies.

- Enjoy getting a new lease on life and experience a sense of freedom and peace. Sleep later than usual and have long, lazy weekends.

- Realize your wish to travel and see more of the world, starting with the many scenic destinations in your own state. The United States has a smorgasbord of fabulous vistas.

This is your time to embrace the new you and fill your life with zest. This stage of life can show parents they have much greater potential than they thought. You may have thought that in rearing your girl you spent yourself, got worn down, and are now coming face-to-face with your own mortality. On the contrary. Now you can discover that you are reawakening and reviving, and you can truly enjoy your realization of immortality: your adult daughter and all she has to offer the world.

Enjoy Your "Masterpiece"

Although your daughter is not a little girl anymore, she continues to crave your love, attention, and acceptance. As always, she wants you to be proud of her now and in the years to come. That means you have to show her that you trust her and that you have faith in her. You have taught her to master the basic life skills and you have instilled good values in her over the years. Now, as she shows by her actions how much she has learned from you, you need to trust in yourself and feel good about all you have done.

Remember this: You were her master teacher throughout her childhood and youth. Although there are many more lessons you can still teach her, as she moves on, take some time to do the following:

○ Relive the wonderful years you had raising your girl.

○ Flip through your photo albums and look at the mementos of the journey.

○ Exhale more deeply than ever before; your biggest job is done!

○ Appreciate the sweet feeling of victory and be grateful that you had the chance to pass on so much of your best—all of it, really!—to your daughter.

Not enough parents pause for long enough to simply rejoice in having done a masterful job in raising their wonderful daughter.

THANKFUL JOB

Here is the most amazing thing: Every minute you concerned yourself with parenting your girl, you did it out of duty, because you loved your child, and because you were her mother or father—and for no other reason. Yet nothing you ever did went unrecorded. Your girl made a mental note of everything. You see, in matters of gratitude a daughter may be quite different than a son. In many cases, she remembers each and every one of the small gestures you made over the years to raise her right.

There is not a single parent of a girl who did not sacrifice something in raising her, but it is not forgotten! Everything you did is etched into the mind and heart of your daughter. While she was growing up, she may not have always been as appreciative as you would have liked, but you can rest assured that you did your best and raised a wonderful young woman.

Celebrate New Traditions

No matter how old your daughter gets, she will always cherish the special occasions you spend together. While family traditions are often passed from generation to generation, do not feel bound by them. You raised the latest version of a great girl, so feel free to adjust old family traditions to fit the new circumstances you find yourself in.

Honor your relationship with your daughter and involve her in deciding how to observe family celebrations and the red-letter days on the calendar. Respect that your daughter is now an adult and before you make any plans involving her, find out:

1. What time she is available. Be willing to shift the celebration to a time more convenient for her.

2. Where she wants to celebrate—at home or in a restaurant, for example—and adjust your plans accordingly.

3. How she wants to celebrate—in a small circle, with the extended family, or by her bringing home a new friend.

Take as much time and effort as possible to make a big deal out of your daughter's birthday, job anniversaries and promotions, college highlights, and special days. The bond you have with your daughter is incredibly strong, but it can still benefit from more golden threads of love woven in.

Celebrating Your Parenting Journey

You celebrate the successful raising of your daughter every day as you look at the framed photo of her that sits on your desk or hangs on the wall, or as you re-read an e-mail or text from her. You also rejoice in your good fortune of having ushered her to her young-adult stage when you tell your friends or neighbors of your girl's latest experiences or escapades on campus or her first few exciting months on the job. Raising a daughter brings a sense of fulfillment and of having been rewarded more than you ever imagined. When you give your daughter the tools to achieve her dream career, handle any competition at work, and be savvy with her money, you infuse her with such power that she will exceed your expectations. In her adult life, she will accomplish many great things because you taught her that nothing is impossible. You did it—you created a living work of art. And along the way, you probably learned a bit about yourself as a parent. By being conscious of your parenting and taking the time to actively reflect on your practices and be purposeful in your daily interactions, you have taken a special journey as well. Congratulations to you!

Appendix A: Bibliography

Biederman, Jerry, and Lorin Biederman, eds. *Parent School: Simple Lessons from the Leading Experts on Being a Mom and Dad* (New York: M. Evans and Co., 2002).

Buchanan, Andrea J., ed. *It's a Girl: Women Writers on Raising Daughters* (Emeryville, CA: Seal Press, 2006).

Chess, Stella, MD, and Alexander Thomas, MD. *Know Your Child* (New York: Basic Books, 1987).

Crick, Nicki R., and Jennifer K. Grotpeter. "Relational Aggression, Gender, and Social-Psychological Adjustment." *Child Development*, Vol. 66, No. 3 (June 1995), pp. 710–722.

Deak, JoAnn, PhD. *Girls Will Be Girls: Raising Confident and Courageous Daughters* (New York: Hyperion, 2002).

Dweck, Carol S., PhD. *Mindset: The New Psychology of Success* (New York: Random House, 2006).

Erwin, Cheryl L., MA, MFT. *The Everything® Parent's Guide to Raising Boys, 2nd Edition* (Avon, MA: Adams Media, 2011).

Felix, Josie. "National Study: New Data Show Teen Girls More Likely to See Benefits in Drug and Alcohol Use." Partnership for Drug-Free Kids (2010) at www.drugfree.org/newsroom/national-study-new-data-show-teen-girls-more-likely-to-see-benefits-in-drug-and-alcohol-use.

Frontline. *Inside the Teenage Brain* (PBS Video, Public Broadcasting Service, 2002).

Gadeberg, Jeanette. *Raising Strong Daughters* (Minneapolis, MN: Fairview Press, 1995).

Harrison, Melissa, and Harry H. Harrison Jr. *Mother to Daughter* (New York: Workman Publishing, 2005).

Hartley-Brewer, Elizabeth. *Raising Confident Girls* (Cambridge, MA: Da Capo Press, 2000).

Healy, Jane M., PhD. *Endangered Minds: Why Children Don't Think and What We Can Do about It* (New York: Touchstone, 1990).

Hersch, Patricia. *A Tribe Apart: A Journey into the Heart of American Adolescence* (New York: Ballantine, 1998).

Holmes, Melisa, MD, and Trish Hutchison, MD. *Girlology: A Girl's Guide to Stuff That Matters* (Deerfield Beach, FL: Health Communications, Inc., 2005).

Karres, Erika V. Shearin, EdD. *Crushes, Flirts, & Friends* (Avon, MA: Adams Media, 2006).

———. *Fab Friends and Best Buds* (Avon, MA: Adams Media, 2005).

———. *Make Your Kids Smarter* (Kansas City, MO: Andrews McMeel Publishing, 2002).

———. *Mean Chicks, Cliques, and Dirty Tricks, 2nd Edition* (Avon, MA: Adams Media, 2010).

———. *Violence Proof Your Kids Now* (Berkeley, CA: Conari Press, 2000).

Neff, Kristin, PhD. *Self-Compassion: The Proven Power of Being Kind to Yourself* (New York: HarperCollins, 2011).

Nelson, Jane, EdD, Cheryl Erwin, MA, and Carol Delzer, MA, JD. *Positive Discipline for Single Parents: Nurturing, Cooperation, Respect, and Joy in Your Single-Parent Family, Revised and Updated 2nd Edition* (New York: Three Rivers Press, 1999).

Norwegian University of Science and Technology. "No Math Gene: Learning Mathematics Takes Practice." EurekAlert! (2013) at www.eurekalert.org/pub_releases/2013-12/nuos-nmg121313.php.

Orenstein, Peggy. *Cinderella Ate My Daughter: Dispatches from the Front Lines of the New Girlie-Girl Culture* (New York: Harper, 2012).

Ricci, Isolina, PhD. *Mom's House, Dad's House: Making Two Homes for Your Child, Revised Edition* (New York: Fireside, 1997).

Siegel, Daniel, MD, and Mary Hartzell, MEd. *Parenting from the Inside Out: How a Deeper Self-Understanding Can Help You Raise Children Who Thrive* (New York: Jeremy P. Tarcher/Penguin, 2003).

Wanless, Shannon B., et al. "Gender Differences in Behavioral Regulation in Four Societies: The U.S., Taiwan, South Korea, and China." Oregon State University Scholars Archive (2013) at http://ir.library.oregonstate.edu/xmlui/handle/1957/38611.

Appendix B: Additional Resources

Parenting Resources

Doing Right By Our Kids
http://doingrightbyourkids.com

Girl Scouts of the USA
www.girlscouts.org

National PTA
www.pta.org

Parents Action for Children
www.parentsaction.org

Positive Discipline Association
www.positivediscipline.org

Tufts University Child & Family WebGuide
www.cfw.tufts.edu

Zero to Three
www.zerotothree.org

Child Care

Child Care Aware
www.childcareaware.org

National Association for the Education of Young Children
www.naeyc.org

Development and Health

Child Development Institute
www.childdevelopmentinfo.com

KidsHealth
www.kidshealth.org

MedlinePlus
www.nlm.nih.gov/medlineplus/parenting.html

Media, Violence, and Culture

A Mighty Girl
www.amightygirl.org

Common Sense Media
www.commonsensemedia.org

Search Institute
www.search-institute.org

Talk with Your Kids
www.talkwithkids.org

Index

false images for, 127–29
fashion and, 168–72
gynecologist visit for, 190–91, 205
healthy bodies, 128–29, 162–66,
    189–205
healthy relationships, 129–30, 189,
    209
Internet safety for, 124–27, 131,
    185–86, 188
media smarts for, 122–24, 131,
    162–63, 172
music/movies and, 127–29
popularity of, 167–68, 172
runaways, 203–4
safety for, 181–84
sexual concerns, 207–18
smoking, 174–81, 188
social media and, 122–27, 131,
    185–86
suicidal thoughts, 197–99
temptations and, 181–83, 188
warning signs in, 173–88
Time-outs/time-ins, 45, 49
Toddler daughter
    curiosity of, 77
    developmental skills, 35–38
    discipline for, 43–45
    following directions, 38–42
    help with, 40
    independence of, 35–38, 48
    listening skills, 38–42
    making choices, 39
    motor skills, 47
    personality of, 40, 47–48
    playdates, 37
    playgroups, 36–37
    play skills, 35–37
    potty training, 47–48
    power struggles with, 35–36
    self-regulation of, 35, 48
    social interactions of, 36–37
    stereotypes, 48–49
    tantrums in, 42–46, 48–49
    television and, 40–41
    toys for, 36–37
    understanding, 38–39

Toys, 25, 36–37, 53–54, 64, 164
Tweens. *See also* School-aged daughter
    abusive boys, 181
    communicating with, 118–20, 188
    crushes, 114
    dangers for, 173–88
    defiant behavior, 117–18
    drinking, 174–81, 188
    drugs, 174–81, 188
    empowering, 97, 113–15
    fashion and, 168–72
    flirting, 114–15
    hormonal changes, 115–17, 120
    Internet safety for, 124–27, 131,
        185–86, 188
    menstruation, 111
    mood swings, 115–17, 120
    popularity of, 167–68, 172
    puberty, 110–17, 120, 129
    rebellious behavior, 117–19
    safety for, 181–84
    secretive behaviors, 118
    sexuality concerns, 112–13
    smoking, 174–81, 188
    social media and, 122–23, 185–86
    temptations and, 181–83, 188
    understanding, 109–20
    warning signs in, 173–88

Warning signs, 173–88
Well-being, 15–16, 189–206. *See also*
    Healthy bodies
Womanhood, 219–30